1 & 2 Samuel

1 & 2 Samuel

RISE OF THE
LORD'S ANOINTED

KAY GABRYSCH

PUBLISHING
P.O. BOX 817 • PHILLIPSBURG • NEW JERSEY 08865-0817

Scripture quotations are from *The ESV Bible*® (*The Holy Bible, English Standard Version*®). Copyright © 2001 by Crossway Bibles, a publishing ministry of Good News Publishers. Used by permission. All rights reserved.

Italics within Scripture quotations indicate emphasis added.

ISBN: 978-1-59638-750-8 (pbk)
ISBN: 978-1-59638-751-5 (ePub)
ISBN: 978-1-59638-752-2 (Mobi)

Printed in the United States of America

To my husband Ray, whose support, patience,
and encouragement are inexhaustible.

Contents

Acknowledgments

WITH DEEP GRATITUDE I give thanks to the faculty and staff of Covenant Theological Seminary. I cannot express in words my great appreciation for the countless hours of online lectures, sermons, and chapel messages that Covenant makes available to any and all students and teachers of the Bible worldwide. Long before I was an actual student at Covenant, I was profoundly impacted through these resources by the teaching of Dr. Bryan Chapell, Dr. Robert Peterson, Dr. Michael Williams, Dr. Dan Doriani, Dr. Phil Long, and others. Listening to their lectures and gleaning from their wisdom had an incalculable influence on my studying and teaching of Scripture. I heartily recommend the use of these beneficial resources to anyone who teaches the Bible, writes Bible studies, or has a desire to dig deeper into the great redemptive truths of the Bible's story.

I wish to thank the women of Park Cities Presbyterian Church in Dallas, Texas, for patiently working through the lessons of a developing Bible study and for always encouraging me to continue writing and teaching. Thank you most of all for praying so faithfully for me. I want to thank Kari Stainback, Director of Women's Ministries, and the pastors of Park Cities for allowing me to try out untested Bible studies on the women of the church.

I especially thank Terri Speicher for her hours, days, and weeks of discerning proofreading, editing, formatting, and correcting, but most importantly for her constant encouragement and enthusiasm for my writing projects.

Thank you to Amanda Martin of P&R Publishing, who is a thorough and gracious editor, and to all others at P&R who contributed to the editing of this study. I thank Dr. David Garner of Westminster Theological Seminary for taking the time to read the study and advise me on it.

Although I have already mentioned him in the list of professors, I want to especially thank Dr. Bryan Chapell for being the teacher of preachers and teachers who first shaped my understanding of how to present a redemptive, Christ-centered message from all Scripture. His teaching is the source of many of the ideas in this study.

Gratitude is due also to the ministry of Bible Study Fellowship, where I first began to study the Bible, came to know and love the Lord Jesus Christ, and received my first structured and disciplined training on teaching and expounding Scripture.

Finally I thank my family, who has always supported my every decision to follow Christ's call in teaching, writing, and now at this late date, obtaining a seminary degree. Thank you for encouraging me and undergirding every effort with your love and prayers.

Introduction

WHEN WE OPEN TO the first page of the New Testament, we read in Matthew 1:18, "Now the birth of Jesus Christ took place in this way." Yet Matthew does not let us come to that great verse nor does he begin to unfold his story of Jesus Christ without first giving us seventeen verses containing a list of names of the ancestors of Christ. It is as if Matthew is telling us that there is no way we will ever understand the story of Jesus Christ properly unless and until we see it in the light of the very long, very old story of the Old Testament, which had been unfolding for centuries and which Christ brings to completion.

From the beginning of Matthew's gospel we are aware that he will demonstrate throughout his story that Jesus is the long-expected Messiah, the Anointed One who is the descendant of the royal line of David and who alone is the rightful heir to David's throne. We can grasp the significance of that claim only if we understand the Old Testament pictures, patterns, and promises of the beginning days of the monarchy, which Jesus fulfills.

The entire Bible is Jesus' story. The Scriptures, beginning with Genesis, tell the ongoing epic tale of God's relentless grace in ransoming his creation through his Son, Jesus Christ. We see in the story of the Bible that God's purpose from creation on was to have a people who would live under his overwhelming blessing in covenant with him. Because of humanity's rebellion against him and man's breaking of that covenant, restoration could only come through God himself. The Old Testament is the story of the people of God repeatedly breaking the covenant of God and God repeatedly coming back in grace to renew it until it is finally and completely fulfilled in his Son, Jesus Christ. Interpreted rightly, the Old Testament prepares us to understand the person and work of the Lord Jesus Christ by showing us how he is the focus of the storyline and the fulfillment of every picture, pattern, symbol, and role. Everything in the New Testament instructs us to see Jesus in the Old. When the risen Christ unfolds the Old Testament to his disciples after their encounter with him on the Emmaus road and shows them how the Scripture is all fulfilled in him, the only reaction they could have in response was to be astonished that they had not seen it before! Like them, we are to see that the central message of the Old Testament is to show us the gospel of Jesus Christ, his suffering, death, resurrection, and reign.

In the history books of 1 and 2 Samuel God establishes an everlasting covenant with David, promising David that one of his descendants will sit on an eternal throne. But despite this glorious promise, the story of David's life demonstrates that even the best of God's anointed earthly kings can sin against God and ignore his promises. This shepherd king who was responsible for defeating God's enemies, for the ongoing welfare of God's people, for establishing true worship of God in Jerusalem, this king rebelled against God in so many ways. It would not be until Jesus Christ came to truly bring his people ultimate good—not to be served as king but to serve, to give his life as a ransom for the true welfare of his people—that God's covenant with David would be fulfilled. Christ, the righteous King, brought lasting peace to his rebellious subjects. Christ is King of Kings, reigning now and forever on the throne of exalted glory. Christ will return from heaven to complete and claim the fullness of his kingdom and to live and reign forever with his people on the earth.

Finally and importantly, the stories of 1 and 2 Samuel are not just records of an inspiring hero king. They are not here to teach us moralistic universal principles of behavior that we can apply to our lives. David's primary function in redemptive history was *not* to model a life by which we could live. David demonstrates that even as he inhabits the role God has given him to further the advancement of God's kingdom on earth, he fails to live up to the righteous rule that God demands of his king. The stories of David's life and reign give us gratitude that our Good Shepherd King has come and truly fulfilled his kingly mission. We have a great privilege and a vast treasure to mine as we study the Old Testament. Jesus mined this same treasure as "morning by morning" he was taught from the Scriptures. The Old Testament was Jesus' Bible. Christopher Wright has said:

I find myself aware that in reading the Hebrew Scriptures I am handling something that gives me a closer common link with Jesus than any archeological artifact could do. For these are the words *he* read. These were the stories *he* knew. These were the songs *he* sang . . . This is where he found *his* insights into the mind of his Father God. Above all, this is where he found the shape of his own identity and the goal of his own mission. In short, the deeper you go into understanding the Old Testament, the closer you come to the heart of Jesus.[1]

This is our glorious privilege as we study, to come ever closer to our King in adoration, love, worship, and obedience.

MINING THE TREASURE

As we study these Old Testament narratives together, we will look at basic literary elements that are common to all of them.

Characterization

Old Testament narrative writers use characterization to move the plotlines of the story along. We will study these characters extensively. Who are they? How do they interact with each other? What is God's evaluation of them? These characters will be revealed both by the narrator's descriptions and by the character's own overt actions and words. Because the stories read like biblical soap operas, you will meet many dysfunctional people. The unvarnished truth about these ancient people is told so that when we see them we will recognize the deceit of our own hearts and see in every narrative how completely God is the hero of every story and how desperately humanity is in need of the righteousness that only God can provide.

Even though David was called "a man after [God's] own heart" (1 Sam. 13:14), he committed adultery and murder and saw his family torn apart by rivalry and chaos. David's story is not a morality play. It is the story of a king who sinned greatly but ultimately chose God's rule instead of his own autonomy. It is the story of a resourceful man who finally depended not on

1. Christopher J. H. Wright, *Knowing Jesus through the Old Testament* (Downers Grove, IL: InterVarsity Press, 1992), ix.

himself but on the faithfulness of God's promise of an eternal King to fully satisfy on his behalf the righteousness that God demands. We know from David's psalms how aware he was of his need of a savior.

The characters of 1 and 2 Samuel encourage and strengthen us as they reveal God breaking into the lives of his people in new ways in response to their need of him.

Because we are part of the family of God made up of people of all times, these stories are memories of *our* past. They inform us, shape our understanding of ourselves, and give us vision and hope for the future. Our Christian faith grows out of confidence in God's dealings with his people in the past. We can rest assured that our unchanging God will act in kind with his people in the present.

Plot Conflict and Resolution

We will see thickening plots filled with tension and conflict throughout the historical narratives. As we read the developing conflict, it will cause us to ask, "How will this turn out?" Just like in any good book or movie, the conflict generates our interest and pushes us through to the resolution.

In every story the conflict will reveal something that is a result of the fall. What is wrong with this person or this situation because of the fall that God must address with grace in order for the wrong to be righted?

What do we see in these ancient peoples' situation as it unfolds that will ultimately require God's intervention and rescue?

God never just brings his people out of the chaos of their sin and then returns them to their former life. His divine resolution always transcends the former situations and keeps them moving forward toward his redemptive goals. That is what makes these stories more than just historical accounts of ancient events and people. The course of events found in 1 and 2 Samuel is placed in the light of an unfolding divine plan. *It is a plan for the rule and reign of God to be visibly established in his creation.*

Application

Because we are seeking not just information but transformation, we will apply these texts to our lives. The Old Testament narratives offer informative and effective implications for our contemporary lives. All of us have misconceptions about God and about ourselves. Old Testament stories present us with proper perspectives on human nature and our sovereign God. It is our responsibility to receive this information and be transformed by the renewing of our minds as we study and apply the truths we will discover. There is one reality by which to interpret our lives and that is God's truth. As we grow in biblical wisdom, we will learn how to rightly apply the truths of Scripture to our lives, and live those truths out in godly ways. We must first ask the primary gospel questions of how is God's work being accomplished in his world, how are we seeing the sins for which Christ had to come and die, and so on, before we can ask, "How then does the gospel teach us to live in light of these truths?" In other words, now that I know the truths contained in this particular passage and understand the gospel better because of this passage, how do I live out of love and gratitude for what God has done? It will be so important to know that, even after we have applied biblical truth to our lives, we must still return to the gospel again and again as we realize that we will never live up to the standard of perfect righteousness that God demands and that only Christ has provided for us. It is because Christians are clothed in *his* perfect righteousness that we can stand before a holy God forgiven.

MEETING THE FAMILY

The two books of Samuel tell of the events in Israel's history from the period of Judges to David's last years. Originally one book, they recount first the story of Samuel, the last of the judges, the transitional figure raised up by God to lead Israel into the period of the monarchy. The stories of his birth and leadership then lead into stories of the first faltering steps of the monarchy under Saul and conclude with David's rise to the throne, along with all the stories of both his covenant failures and covenant faithfulness.

Many scholars believe that the audience for this portion of Scripture would most likely have been the nation of Israel in exile. The book probably reached its final form just prior to or during the exile. The books of 1 and 2 Samuel and 1 and 2 Kings explain to the exiles why they are in captivity—because of the unfaithfulness of the Davidic monarchy. David's family had led the people of Israel astray many times, and the blame for the exile fell largely on David's house (2 Kings 21:10–15). But despite the moral failure of the human kings, Israel's hope was and always would be in the ultimate Son of David, a Messianic King who would sit on the throne of a gloriously restored Israel. In expectation the exiles and all true Israelites after them listened, and in hope they clung to the stories of their covenant God and his promises to his people to have an everlasting king on David's throne.

REACHING THE GOAL

The Bible is God condescending to speak to his people in ways we can hear and understand if we will carefully and attentively listen. In hearing, comprehending, and responding there is great reward. It is not just God's Word. It is God's Word given for and to his people. If you listen and ask the Holy Spirit to be your teacher, you have his promise that you will hear. The Scripture discloses God's will for us. It sheds light on and publishes God's norms for all of life in his world. It offers us a corrective lens and gives us warnings, commands, promises, callings, and comfort. But most importantly, it and it alone can bring us to a saving knowledge of the Lord Jesus Christ. Through Scripture alone we are brought to faith in Christ. Through Scripture alone the Holy Spirit breaks through our confusion and clearly shows us the one true King. God does not leave us on our own to figure it out. He gives us his own Holy Spirit to read it to us and interpret it for us. Through Scripture alone our hearts are changed, and we respond to Christ in adoration, thankfulness, love, and obedience.

Overview

THE BIBLE STUDY METHOD

If you are doing this study as a member of a Bible study group, each week you will read, study, and answer questions on your own in your personal study time before coming to discuss the lesson as part of a discussion group.

This study has been designed to give us tools of biblical interpretation that will make us more careful readers of Scripture. You will find that as the weeks go by and you follow the format of the questions and interact with others, interpretive skills will begin to grow. You will become more comfortable each week with the lessons as you learn to become a more careful reader of Scripture. Focus on what you are able to do in the beginning and do not be discouraged by that which is left undone. Your study efforts will become more and more fruitful as you become more and more familiar with the method of this study, which calls for careful observation of the text, asking questions of the text, and meditating on the text.

YOUR APPROACH TO BIBLE STUDY

The most important thing to do before you begin your lesson each day is to pray for the Holy Spirit to open your mind to what he has to teach you and to enlarge your heart with love for Jesus Christ through what you will learn. Many verses in the Psalms are helpful prayers for a teachable heart, such as Psalm 119:18: "Open my eyes, that I may behold wondrous things out of your law." The Bible is not just God's Word; it is God's Word to his people, and he attends to it by his Spirit.

He *wants* us to hear what he is saying to his people. The Spirit teaches, illuminates, and penetrates our hearts with the Word. Set aside time each day to really study the passage, and you will be encouraged by the ways in which the Spirit of God will speak to you through his authoritative, powerful, and all-sufficient Word.

BIG PICTURE QUESTIONS

Every week we will look at big-picture, general questions designed to be asked of each passage. These questions will not change from week to week. Always some—and often all—these questions will be applicable to every story in 1 and 2 Samuel. In the first lesson, you will be given explanations to guide you and stimulate your thought processes for each of these questions. You may want to refer back to the first lesson's explanations to inform your thoughts as you answer the questions in subsequent lessons. Each week you will also answer a limited number of questions that are exclusive to the particular passage being studied. These questions are designed to focus your thoughts on a main idea of the passage.

THE ULTIMATE GOAL

Here are just a few things to consider about the kingdom then and now. The books of 1 and 2 Samuel are concerned with a particular period of Israel's history—the rise of the monarchy. All the narratives relate events that took place during the period in which God was establishing what had always been a factor in his plans for his people—the earthly monarchy. The world for God's people changed with the monarchy, and their relationship with God would forever after be defined by their relationship with God's anointed king. The earthly monarchy, with all its weaknesses, was intended to clearly demonstrate the necessity of the perfect embodiment of God's king. The monarchy was a gracious gift of God to his chosen people that organized his kingdom under a human, earthly ruler. But it was so much more.

God's kingdom under David would point to and be a pattern for the coming kingdom that would be established by the King of Kings, the Lord Jesus Christ. David's establishment of a kingdom in which God's enemies were defeated, worship was at the forefront of life, and there was unity among the people of Israel was a type, a pattern, of the kingdom of the one true King who would eventually come and reign, putting all God's enemies under his feet and establishing peace forever. Everything about it was supposed to point to and prepare God's people to recognize his true King when he came.

But even though Israel hoped throughout the ages for the Messiah who would come to inaugurate God's kingdom, when Jesus finally came he was not the kind of king Israel was expecting. He was not the warrior-ruler David had been. He did not drive out the physical enemies of God and place himself on a physical throne in earthly Jerusalem. Instead he transformed lives and changed hearts by driving out the spiritual enemies of God's people; and instead of being enthroned in Jerusalem, he was nailed to a cross outside the city. He gave his life in payment for the sins of his people and rose from the dead for their justification. To all who would put their faith in him, he gave the gift of eternal life and the promise that they are spiritually secure until he comes again; they are protected, sealed, and defended by the Lion of Judah who is also the Lamb who was slain and who by his death and resurrection has victoriously overcome his enemy.

God's people are already kingdom citizens, living in the age between Christ's two comings, living in the kingdom that he has already inaugurated by his first coming. That kingdom has been ushered in and is growing in the midst of a hostile world while Christ sovereignly rules from his heavenly throne. While we live as kingdom citizens and wait for his return, we are to understand that our enemies are real and to see them in their true colors. But we are never to lose sight of our champion as he sits enthroned in his true glory, ruling every square inch of his universe. We are to trust, love, and serve him, our Lord Jesus Christ, who has defeated Satan at the cross and who will one day come back to send him into his eternal punishment. We are to worship and adore him who is seated on God's throne in power, who like his father David went out in the name of the Lord to fight the enemies of God's people and conquered. Christ is the one who is right now the ruling warrior general of heaven's armies and who will come again in his holy wrath to destroy all that defiles his creation and sets itself up against his church.

The great heritage of the Old Testament narratives of David's reign gives us glimpses and pictures and patterns of who Christ is and what he came to do. Christ himself is the key to our interpretation of David's story. Over and over again David shows us why only God in flesh could ever be the answer to our deepest need. Jesus Christ is the true King who stepped into history and plunged headlong into the battle and poured out his life in order to have his people with him forever. May this study help you see him as victorious King and serve him as his loving ambassador in the midst of a hostile world until he comes and brings the glory of heaven to earth.

LESSON 1

1 Samuel 1:1–2:10

MEDITATION AND DISCOVERY

1. Read the entire passage and, as you read, observe the details of the settings, situations, and crises of peoples' lives. Circle or write down repeated words that highlight the narrator's emphasis. The writers of Hebrew narratives use repetition to emphasize character traits, action, theological points, etc. Next, look for contrasting words like *darkness/light, strength/weakness*, etc. The words *but* and *yet* will often signal a contrast as well. Next, look for words that signal time and scene changes, such as *then* and *now*.

2. Write down questions that come to mind that you expect or hope will be answered as you study. These might include but are certainly not limited to:

    • What does this particular thing mean?
    • Where is this happening?
    • Why are they doing this particular thing?
    • What surprises you in the story?

    Good interpretation involves asking many questions of the text!

3. Next we will look at the context of the passage. What precedes and follows this passage, and what light do these "next-door neighbors" shed on the passage? Determine how this particular passage fits into the central idea of all 1 and 2 Samuel. Expand the context to the whole Bible. Where does the passage/book fit into the whole story of Scripture? What was going on historically at the time this was written? Who made up the original audience? Two very important keys to interpretation are (1) what was the author's intent in writing to his audience? and (2) what would that original audience have understood?

Rule #1: Relax! Understanding a passage in its context is not something that can be done up front if you are not familiar with the Old Testament, but it is so important to understanding the text. It will become easier for you as you go along in this study and understand more and more the "one-story-ness" of the Bible.

Each book of the Bible is a link in the chain of the progressive, unfolding, larger story of redemption. God progressively and coherently tells his story over thousands of years. The Bible is not just a collection of truth statements. It is held together by a storyline. It is best understood as a narrative. It is the story of God, who has created a world in which the apex of his creation, humankind, has rebelled against him, thus creating the conflict for which God provides the resolution, his Son, Jesus Christ. It is a story of creation, rebellion, redemption, and re-creation. The beginnings of the monarchy have an important and specific part in that unfolding story.

4. After reading and rereading the passage, what do you think is the main idea or theme of this particular passage?

CHARACTERIZATION AND SCENES

Because the story of redemption begins with the Old Testament and is told from Genesis to Revelation, God makes himself known in the Old Testament stories in his covenant relationships to his people and in his relationships to all his creation. The God who redeemed Hannah, Samuel, and David is the same God of all grace who has redeemed those in the New Testament. The means by which God has worked in history has always been human beings living in time and space.

When we read the stories of God's ancient people, we are reading the stories of our own spiritual ancestors who have gone before us and played their parts on the stage of God's drama. How humbling to see how tiny our lives are in the enormous scheme of things, yet how dignifying to have a role to play in that scheme. When we belong to God through faith in Christ, we can know that we are enabled by his Spirit to walk like those who have gone before us and to take our place as a participant in the story as each of them did. As Dr. Michael Williams likes to say, "We are not the trees in the school play." We have a role to faithfully inhabit and a contribution to make to the establishing of Christ's kingdom as we live in these times between Christ's first and second comings.

When we study the characters of the historical narratives, we see that our relational God cares deeply about his people and is constantly involved in their lives for his glory and their good. Every character in the story is defined by his or her relationship to God. Notice that they are real people with conflicts, choices, sins, consequences, joys, and sorrows. They are people just like us who face each day not knowing what it will bring. Some will be grappling with suffering, some will be acting on the sin in their hearts, some will be living in accordance with the purposes of God. Be on the lookout for how God confirms the identity of those who are his—comforting, disciplining, and providentially working in and through them, always for their good and his glory. Conversely, identify how he confronts the many ways in which people turn away from the character and ways of God in complete rebellion.

The Bible is a story about what God has *done* to redeem his sin-sick world. He is not just the sum of attributes and names to be memorized and studied. He is always *acting* in relationship with his people. Consequently the fundamental question will always be: what is God doing in these people's lives and in his world in this part of the story to drive the story forward toward its ultimate goal—the coming of the Lord Jesus Christ in his life, death, resurrection, and reign both in this age and the age to come?

1. Make a list of characters and identify habits, desires, emotions, overt actions, and speech of each that give clues to their relationship to God and the condition of their hearts. According to the narrator, what is God's evaluation of their conduct and character?

2. As they dialogue and interact with each other, how are the characters in this passage contributing to each other's lives? Contrast the positive traits of some characters with the negative traits of others. Notice the ways the darkness of some characters accentuates the brilliance of others.

3. In no other genre does our attention so easily drift from God to human beings than in Old Testament narratives. Therefore it is crucial that we constantly ask ourselves, "What does God reveal about himself here?" No matter who the human characters are in the story, we must always see that God is the hero of every passage. We are always looking for how the telling of the story is depicting God, his character, his values, and his mission for those in the story and those to whom the story was told. The intensity of God's presence will vary from passage to passage. In some passages he will interact extensively with his creatures, speaking and directing events in the heart of the action. In some he will be less explicit, and it will appear as if human actions dominate, even as he is providentially controlling all events.

Thoughts to guide you as you consider what you are learning about God in this passage:

• Where do you see him confronting people in truth, power, compassion, grace, mercy, judgment, etc.?

- Where do you see him acting in mercy for the guilty, strength for the weak, love for the unlovely and undeserving, provision for the needy, warning for those who are in error, punishment for enemies, and rescue of his people from enemies from whom they cannot rescue themselves?
- Where do you see discipline that turns people back into God's arms and away from unsafe paths?
- Keeping these examples in mind, what evidences of his grace and attributes of his character are predominately on display in this particular passage?

4. What inconsistency or error in your thinking about God is corrected by seeing his involvement with the characters in this story?

5. What are the prominent concerns and issues in these characters' lives with which you most identify? Why?

6. Make two lists: one list of the issues involved in this ancient situation, and another list of what might be the contemporary equivalents of those issues.

Ancient Issue	Contemporary Equivalent

QUESTIONS ON 1 SAMUEL 1:1-2:10

We must see this story in the context of Israel's unfolding history and God's plan to send the true and perfect King before we can understand the significance of the answered prayer of this humble, obscure woman. Hannah arrived on the scene when the nation was spiritually crumbling. The priesthood was corrupt, the people were indifferent to God and, as Judges reminds us over and over, "In those days there was no king in Israel. Everyone did what was right in his own eyes" (Judg. 17:6; 21:25). All of a sudden, the biblical narrative zeroes in on the painful marriage and barren womb of one woman.

Look carefully at Hannah's story and how God uses this insignificant, barren woman to bring about his redemptive plans. While we struggle to understand this God who seems to be withholding the very blessings we crave, he is using the struggle to reveal to us his greater purposes in our own life's story and in his kingdom.

Chapter 1

1. Like so many women before her, Hannah finds herself in the heartbreaking condition of barrenness.

   Read Genesis 25:20–21, 26; 29:31; 30:22–23. In light of the extraordinary promise the Lord made to the woman in Genesis 3:15 regarding her role in the redemptive plan, every Israelite woman knew that it was important and necessary to have children. One of the blessings of the Mosaic covenant was that "the fruit of your womb" would be blessed (Deut. 28:4). How would Hannah have been perceived within the Israelite community, as seen in Peninnah's treatment of her?

In light of the covenant promise of blessing, what is Hannah really yearning for?

2. As he often does, God chooses to begin the story of the next phase of redemptive history with what appears to be a hopeless situation. What other new chapter of redemptive history begins with a barren woman who has prayed for a child for many years? Read Luke 1:5–7.

3. What are the similarities between Hannah's story and Elizabeth's story and between the roles that Hannah's child and Elizabeth's child would play in God's unfolding plan? (See 1 Samuel 8:4–7; John 3:27–30.)

4. Who is responsible for Hannah's barrenness (vv. 1–8)? How does knowing that affect Hannah's confidence in God?

5. There is a well-known little phrase that says, "If you ask the wrong thing, God says, 'No.' If you ask the right thing at the wrong time, God says, 'Go slow.'" Hannah has been asking for the right thing, but God has "gone slowly" for quite a while until the unique time God chooses to bring about his purposes. Read Luke 18:1–7. What is Jesus teaching about God in this parable that Hannah already seems to know?

6. Hannah's logic in prayer is based on her assumption that God cares about an anxiety-ridden, afflicted woman in a stressful marriage. What does the faithful remnant of Israel, of which Hannah was a part, know about Yahweh that we also are to know? (See Exodus 3:7–8a.)

7. Once Eli determines that Hannah is not drunk, but desperate, he blesses her with an assurance that the God of Israel has heard her prayer. The true Israelite like Hannah would believe the word of God spoken through the mediation of a priest. What is her reaction to that assurance from God spoken through her mediator, Eli?

Read Hebrews 8:1–2 and John 17. How often do you finish your prayers in this assurance that your perfect heavenly Mediator has heard your prayer? What would it look like in your life today if you were resting in the assurance of his intercession on your behalf that these passages give?

8. Is Hannah's main focus in her relationship with God his granting of her own personal longings, or is her prayer within the context of God's will, glory, and vindication? How do you know which one it is?

9. Hannah makes a vow to God that she will give her son to the Lord for service as a Nazarite. (See Numbers 6:1–5.) When the time comes to give Samuel up, Elkanah participates in Hannah's act of obedience. What can we learn about Elkanah from this? (See Numbers 30:3–8.)

3. What stories precede and follow this passage, and what light do these "next-door neighbors" shed on the passage? Determine how this particular passage fits into the central idea of all 1 and 2 Samuel. Expand the context to the whole Bible. How does the passage fit into the whole story of Scripture? What was the author's intent, and what would the original audience have understood?

4. After reading and rereading the passage, what do you think is the main idea or theme of this particular passage?

CHARACTERIZATION AND SCENES

1. Make a list of characters and identify habits, desires, emotions, overt actions, and speech of each that give clues to their relationship to God and what is in their hearts. What is God's evaluation of their conduct and character?

2. As they dialogue and interact with each other, how are the characters in this passage contributing to each other's lives? Contrast the positive traits of some characters with the negative traits of

others. Notice the ways the darkness of some characters accentuates the brilliance of others.

3. In no other genre does our attention so easily drift from God to human beings than in Old Testament narratives. Therefore it is crucial that we constantly ask ourselves, "What does God reveal about himself here?"

Thoughts to guide you:

- Where do you see him confronting people in truth, power, compassion, grace, mercy, judgment, etc.?
- Where do you see him acting in mercy for the guilty, strength for the weak, love for the unlovely and undeserving, provision for the needy, warning for those who are in error, punishment for enemies, and rescue of his people from enemies from whom they cannot rescue themselves?
- Where do you see discipline that turns people back into God's arms and away from unsafe paths?
- Keeping these examples in mind, what evidences of his grace and attributes of his character are predominately on display in this particular passage?

(Continued from previous page)

4. What inconsistency or error in your thinking about God is corrected by seeing his involvement with the characters in this story?

5. What are the prominent concerns and issues in these characters' lives with whom you most identify? Why?

6. Make two lists: one list of the issues involved in this ancient situation, and another list of what might be the contemporary equivalents of those issues.

ANCIENT ISSUE	CONTEMPORARY EQUIVALENT

QUESTIONS ON 1 SAMUEL 4:1B–7:17

Chapter 4

1. The first scenes make clear which military force is more powerful. After Israel's massive defeat, what explanation was given for it by the elders, and what would be their next strategy?

2. Dale Ralph Davis says, "Whenever the church stops confessing *Thou art worthy* and begins thinking *Thou art useful*, well then you know the ark of God has been captured again."[1] What has the ark always meant to the people of God? (See Exodus 25:22.)

What do the Israelite leaders misunderstand about God's power and presence when they send for the ark? How do we see his

1. Dale Ralph Davis, *1 Samuel: Looking on the Heart* (Fearn, Great Britain: Christian Focus, 2000), 55.

power and presence being misunderstood by people today? What are some of the erroneous ways people like to think about God? For example, "I like to think of God as . . . "

3. How many times in chapter 4 is the capture of the ark of God mentioned, and how does Eli's daughter-in-law sum up how catastrophic this is for the people of God?

4. God had told Eli that he would judge the ungodly leadership of Eli's house. What was to be the sign of this judgment? (See 1 Samuel 2:31–34.)

What can we learn about God's promises of judgment in this passage?

Chapter 5

Chapter 5 describes what is almost a victory tour of the ark of the covenant of the Lord. The ark travels from one Philistine city to another as Yahweh terrorizes Israel's greatest enemy.

5. Verses 1–5 relate one of Scripture's most amusing scenes. However, whenever a scene in Scripture appears comical, you can be sure it is also deadly serious. What very serious point is the writer making with the humor in this scene? (See Isaiah 46:1–13.)

6. The use of the word *hand* is a literary motif in this passage. The Philistines originally thought that the ark of God had been defeated and fallen into their hands. The next thing they know, their god has lost his hands. By the time the ark reaches the last Philistine city, whose hand is seen to be in control, and what word is used to describe that hand?

The same Hebrew word is used in 4:21–22 for *glory*, when Eli's daughter-in-law proclaims that the glory has left Israel. What can you learn about God's glory from this use of the word to describe his hand of judgment?

Chapter 6

7. The consensus of the Philistines is clear: the ark must go back to Israel! What has happened in world history that is impacting the Philistines' thinking? Read Exodus 12:29–36 and comment on the similarities between the two situations.

What can we learn from Exodus 14:18, 31 about why God would allow the ark to be captured?

8. After the ark arrives safely back in Israelite territory in the village of Beth-shemesh, divine retribution continues to overtake those who misuse it. Read verses 13–20. Why does God strike down these men? (See also Numbers 4:5, 20.)

Our culture wants us to see God as a "casual god," the essence of tolerance. There is a belief that we can come to God on our own terms, whatever they may be. But the clear message from Genesis to Revelation is that "it is a fearful thing to fall into the hands of the living God" (Heb. 10:31). When we fall into his hands because we have despaired of everything else in which we have trusted, we will find mercy. But if we come to him on our own invented terms, we will meet the God who judges. Only when we come to God through his appointed Mediator will we experience his goodness, grace, and fatherhood.

In the Old Testament God is always establishing his patterns for approaching him and finding intimacy with him. When we see him discipline his people for inventing their own methods of approaching him, we are meant to examine our own lives for ways in which we too might be trusting in our own superstitious efforts instead of resting our whole confidence on our ascended King and Mediator who intercedes on our behalf. We cannot approach this God unless we approach him completely clothed in the righteousness of Christ and confident that his efforts alone have won our acceptance before the Father.

Chapter 7

After being absent from the narrative in chapters 4–6, Samuel reenters the scene. The ark is now in the care of a consecrated man who will be in charge of it for many years.

9. This four-chapter passage begins and ends with a contrast between faithless and faithful leadership, a theme that runs throughout the books of Samuel. Now faithful Samuel steps forward to call the nation to repentance. He commands the Israelites to put out of their lives anything that is opposed to the way of life of the people of God and the commandments he has given them. What particular things are demanded of them if they are to show full repentance?

10. At this time the people of Israel are enveloped in idol worship. It has been said that an idol cannot be removed; it must be replaced. According to verses 3–4 and Colossians 3:1–10, what is the only effective replacement?

11. The chapters we have studied are bookended by Philistine-Israelite battles with very different outcomes. Toward the end of the story, the Philistines hear of the gathering of the nation and come to attack the Israelites. The Philistines are still the superior military force, but this time the Israelite strategy is radically different from the opening battle in chapter 4. What will be her weapons of war this time?

12. After the return of the ark and the repentance of the people, the blessings of God flow to Israel. List the blessings seen in verses 12–14, and then compare those blessings with those of Christians in Romans 5:1–2.

13. It is Yahweh who puts the superior military force of Israel's greatest enemy to shame. How does Colossians 2:13–15 tell us that the Lord Jesus Christ defeated his people's greatest enemy in this same way?

14. It is sometimes difficult for us to understand why God allows certain things. For instance, although the ark was the symbol of his dwelling with his people, he allowed his glory and his presence represented by the ark to be taken into captivity and dishonored. Read John 1:14. Now read John 19:1–3, 16–24 along with Philippians 2:5–11. What was the ultimate humiliation of God's presence and glory?

53

CONFLICT AND RESOLUTION

1. Where in this story do you see God's people recognizing what their sin deserves, seeing their need of grace, and desperately longing for a divine solution and new life?

2. How do you see the breaking in of the glorious good news of God's provision of the removal of our sin and guilt through the perfect substitute of Jesus Christ's death and resurrection?

APPLICATION

We study Old Testament narratives and all Scripture on a spiritual battlefield. We are constantly pulled back and forth between sinful and righteous living, between self-effort and humble dependence on Christ in us. After studying this passage, ask God to cause you to see with heightened sensitivity what the Holy Spirit wants you to implement in your own life. The application questions we will answer bring us to the "so what?" question. *Why is this passage here? What does God want me to learn/change about me?*

1. What are the ways in which submission to God has taken place in this passage? Where in your own life does it need to take place?

2. What are the ways in which the flesh (selfish desires, manipulation, etc.) has won out in this passage, and how is that showing up in your own life as a need for repentance?

3. Think about how relationship to God has been broken in this passage (due to sin, immaturity, doubt, trial, suffering, etc.). In view of the events in this passage, in what ways does Christ's victory over temptation, sin, and death bring hope, joy, and strength to your walk of faith today?

4. Where in your life will you look for God's gracious provision for your need, forgiveness for your sin, strength in your weakness, discipline or correction as you have seen it here in these lives?

5. What are the truths about God and his rule that you have learned that cause you to rejoice and trust him more?

6. Finally, always in application, ask yourself these three questions:

- *What* does God require of me as a result of having learned the truths of this passage?

- *Where* in my life do I need to do it? What specific area of my life needs this implementation?

- *Why* and *how* can I do it? We will answer this one together. The power of the resurrected, ascended Lord Jesus Christ indwells his people. It is by him, through him, and for him that you are enabled to obey. The compulsion of grace causes us to want to obey and grow in holiness. He sets us apart to holiness when he saves us by a powerful working of his Spirit in our lives that enables us to live for him. The Westminster Confession, chapter 16, says, "Good works done in obedience to God's commandments are the fruits and evidences of a true and lively faith, but a Christian's ability to do good works is not at all of themselves but wholly of the Spirit of Christ."

We must recognize in some way every passage points not only to our need of redemption, but also to God's provision of our redemption, including his enabling, powerful Holy Spirit. The Bible is not a self-help book. "Apart from me you can do nothing," Jesus said (John 15:5).

Pray that the Holy Spirit will cause us to consider what to fight, where to fight, why to fight, and how to fight anything that comes against that growth in holiness.

LESSON 4

1 Samuel 8–10

AN EARTHLY MONARCHY had always been God's plan for his people. The very heart of the idea of a monarchy is seen in the reign of God from the time of creation until the great consummation and into eternity. God is King. The very word *sovereignty* means rule. The human king who exercised godly authority over God's people foreshadowed the ultimate reign on earth of the divine King, God himself, who came in flesh.

The reign of a king over the nation of Israel was not a new idea to the people at this time. In Genesis 17:6 God had told Abraham that kings would be his descendants. In Deuteronomy 17:14–20 Moses had outlined the divine expectations that Israel's kings were to meet.

But always, from the beginning, it was to be recognized that God is ultimately King and that he alone possesses ultimate authority and power. If there was to be a king of Israel—and there would be many— each one would have to recognize that he was to rule Israel under the sovereign authority of God. This is the foundational premise by which we are to understand the narratives of the monarchy.

MEDITATION AND DISCOVERY

1. Read the entire passage and, as you read, become aware of the details of the settings, situations, and crises of peoples' lives. Circle or write down repeated words that will highlight the narrator's emphasis. Circle or write down contrasting words. Circle or write down scene-changing words.

2. Write down questions that come to mind that you expect or hope will be answered as you study. These might include but are certainly not limited to:

   • What does this particular thing mean?
   • Where is this happening?
   • Why are they doing this particular thing?
   • What surprises you in the story?

   Good interpretation involves asking many questions of the text!

3. What stories precede and follow this passage, and what light do these "next-door neighbors" shed on the passage? Determine how this particular passage fits into the central idea of all 1 and 2 Samuel. Expand the context to the whole Bible. How does the passage fit into the whole story of Scripture? What was the author's intent, and what would the original audience have understood?

4. After reading and rereading the passage, what do you think is the main idea or theme of this particular passage?

CHARACTERIZATION AND SCENES

1. Make a list of characters and identify habits, desires, emotions, overt actions, and speech of each that give clues to their relationship to God and what is in their hearts. What is God's evaluation of their conduct and character?

2. As they dialogue and interact with each other, how are the characters in this passage contributing to each other's lives? Contrast the positive traits of some characters with the negative traits of

others. Notice the ways the darkness of some characters accentuates the brilliance of others.

3. In no other genre does our attention so easily drift from God to human beings than in Old Testament narratives. Therefore it is crucial that we constantly ask ourselves, "What does God reveal about himself here?"

Thoughts to guide you:

- Where do you see him confronting people in truth, power, compassion, grace, mercy, judgment, etc.?
- Where do you see him acting in mercy for the guilty, strength for the weak, love for the unlovely and undeserving, provision for the needy, warning for those who are in error, punishment for enemies, and rescue of his people from enemies from whom they cannot rescue themselves?
- Where do you see discipline that turns people back into God's arms and away from unsafe paths?
- Keeping these examples in mind, what evidences of his grace and attributes of his character are predominately on display in this particular passage?

3. What stories precede and follow this passage, and what light do these "next-door neighbors" shed on the passage? Determine how this particular passage fits into the central idea of all 1 and 2 Samuel. Expand the context to the whole Bible. How does the passage fit into the whole story of Scripture? What was the author's intent, and what would the original audience have understood?

4. After reading and rereading the passage, what do you think is the main idea or theme of this particular passage?

CHARACTERIZATION AND SCENES

1. Make a list of characters and identify habits, desires, emotions, overt actions, and speech of each that give clues to their relationship to God and what is in their hearts. What is God's evaluation of their conduct and character?

2. As they dialogue and interact with each other, how are the characters in this passage contributing to each other's lives? Contrast the positive traits of some characters with the negative traits of

others. Notice the ways the darkness of some characters accentuates the brilliance of others.

3. In no other genre does our attention so easily drift from God to human beings than in Old Testament narratives. Therefore it is crucial that we constantly ask ourselves, "What does God reveal about himself here?"

Thoughts to guide you:

- Where do you see him confronting people in truth, power, compassion, grace, mercy, judgment, etc.?
- Where do you see him acting in mercy for the guilty, strength for the weak, love for the unlovely and undeserving, provision for the needy, warning for those who are in error, punishment for enemies, and rescue of his people from enemies from whom they cannot rescue themselves?
- Where do you see discipline that turns people back into God's arms and away from unsafe paths?
- Keeping these examples in mind, what evidences of his grace and attributes of his character are predominately on display in this particular passage?

(Continued from previous page)

4. What inconsistency or error in your thinking about God is cor-
    rected by seeing his involvement with the characters in this story?

5. What are the prominent concerns and issues in these characters'
    lives with whom you most identify? Why?

6. Make two lists: one list of the issues involved in this ancient situation, and another list of what might be the contemporary equivalents of those issues.

ANCIENT ISSUE	CONTEMPORARY EQUIVALENT

QUESTIONS ON 1 SAMUEL 13–14

Saul's first act as king is to set up a standing army made up of troops that he has chosen and on whose competence he will rely. He will command two divisions, and his son Jonathan, having the authority to act on the king's behalf, will command one. Prior to the monarchy, Israel relied on citizen militia under the leadership of whichever judge God raised up to lead in times of crisis.

After Jonathan's defeat of a Philistine stronghold and Saul's spreading of the word of victory, the Israelite men join him in support at Gilgal. The effect of this on the Philistines is to cause them to mobilize in even greater numbers with their superior military might. At this point, the Philistines strike such fear in the Israelites that the newly mustered Israelite armies begin to flee and hide. As Saul waits for Samuel at Gilgal, the men who are left with him are scared and scattering.

Chapter 13

1. Look back at Samuel's initial, very specific instructions to Saul in 10:7–8, which would have been procedure before a battle. It seems as though Saul may have waited *until* the appointed day but not *through* the appointed day (v. 10a). Samuel's point in this dialogue is that Saul knows perfectly well what instructions he has been given in this situation. If God's word has been clearly stated, what then is Saul's excuse?

   Is there ever an adequate explanation for not doing God's revealed will?

2. Dale Ralph Davis says, "For Saul, sacrificial ritual was essential but prophetic direction dispensable."[1] What is God's view of those who carry out rituals but have no heart for God? (See Isaiah 1:12–18.) What does Jesus have to say about this attitude? (See Matthew 23:23.)

3. Look back at verse 12. By his own admission, what has Saul failed to do that he could have done privately without disobedience?

4. The condemnation and penalty Samuel decrees for Saul is severe: the loss of his kingdom. What is Samuel establishing about the office of an Israelite king that would distinguish him from the kings of other nations?

1. Davis, *1 Samuel*, 136.

5. The Hebrew word for *heart* describes not so much the emotions as the will, the thinking, and the planning of a person. God calls the next king "a man after his own heart" (13:14). In light of Saul's condemnation, what do you think that phrase means, and what does it tell us about Saul as well as David?

6. The rest of chapter 13 depicts the superiority of the Philistines in weaponry and military skill. The Israelites are still living in the Bronze Age, while the Philistines, who came from the Aegean regions, have access to iron, which they monopolized. What is the result of this monopoly on the smaller, tribal Israelite armies?

Chapter 14

7. Contrast Jonathan's statement of faith in verse 6 with what we have just seen in his father's attitude in chapter 13.

8. The sudden attack of Jonathan and his armor-bearer creates confusion in the Philistine camp. Such noise and chaos gets the attention of Saul and brings him into the battle. The Philistines are routed as "the LORD save[s] Israel that day" (v. 23) but, after an entire day of fierce fighting, Saul's men are completely physically exhausted from lack of food. Who is responsible for the Israelites' dire physical condition?

What does Jesus say about rash oaths taken to demonstrate false piety? (See Matthew 5:33–37.)

9. So much of the attractiveness of Jonathan is contrasted with the darkness of Saul in order that we may see clearly the complete unsuitability of Saul to be king. When Jonathan hears that he has in ignorance violated his father's oath, what is his reaction, and how does it further demonstrate the contrast between him and his father?

10. Even though Saul is painted for most of his reign in a negative light, verses 47–52 are a positive summary of his actions. By human, observable standards, Saul has been successful. Many of the leaders of the Bible's story are observable successes in people's eyes and covenantal failures in God's. What is lacking in the first king of Israel that keeps him from living up to God's ideal for his people? (See John 15:4–6.)

11. The monarchs of Israel were charged with faithful obedience to Yahweh the King under whom they reigned on earth. Who is the only King of Israel to fully carry out that mandate, and how, in his own words, did he do that? (See John 5:19, 30.)

CONFLICT AND RESOLUTION

1. Where in this story do you see God's people recognizing what their sin deserves, seeing their need of grace, and desperately longing for a divine solution and new life?

2. How do you see the breaking in of the glorious good news of God's provision of the removal of our sin and guilt through the perfect substitute of Jesus Christ's death and resurrection?

APPLICATION

We study Old Testament narratives and all Scripture on a spiritual battlefield. We are constantly pulled back and forth between sinful and righteous living, between self-effort and humble dependence on Christ in us. After studying this passage, ask God to cause you to see with heightened sensitivity what the Holy Spirit wants you to implement in your own life. The application questions we will answer bring us to the "so what?" question. *Why is this passage here? What does God want me to learn/change about me?*

1. What are the ways in which submission to God has taken place in this passage? Where in your own life does it need to take place?

2. What are the ways in which the flesh (selfish desires, manipulation, etc.) has won out in this passage, and how is that showing up in your own life as a need for repentance?

3. Think about how relationship to God has been broken in this passage (due to sin, immaturity, doubt, trial, suffering, etc.). In view of the events in this passage, in what ways does Christ's victory over temptation, sin, and death bring hope, joy, and strength to your walk of faith today?

4. Where in your life will you look for God's gracious provision for your need, forgiveness for your sin, strength in your weakness, discipline or correction as you have seen it here in these lives?

5. What are the truths about God and his rule that you have learned that cause you to rejoice and trust him more?

6. Finally, always in application, ask yourself these three questions:

- *What* does God require of me as a result of having learned the truths of this passage?

- *Where* in my life do I need to do it? What specific area of my life needs this implementation?

- *Why* and *how* can I do it? We will answer this one together. The power of the resurrected, ascended Lord Jesus Christ indwells his people. It is by him, through him, and for him that you are enabled to obey. The compulsion of grace causes us to want to obey and grow in holiness. He sets us apart to holiness when he saves us by a powerful working of his Spirit in our lives that enables us to live for him. The Westminster Confession, chapter 16, says, "Good works done in obedience to God's commandments are the fruits and evidences of a true and lively faith, but a Christian's ability to do good works is not at all of themselves but wholly of the Spirit of Christ."

3. What stories precede and follow this passage, and what light do these "next-door neighbors" shed on the passage? Determine how this particular passage fits into the central idea of all 1 and 2 Samuel. Expand the context to the whole Bible. How does the passage fit into the whole story of Scripture? What was the author's intent, and what would the original audience have understood?

4. After reading and rereading the passage, what do you think is the main idea or theme of this particular passage?

CHARACTERIZATION AND SCENES

1. Make a list of characters and identify habits, desires, emotions, overt actions, and speech of each that give clues to their relationship to God and what is in their hearts. What is God's evaluation of their conduct and character?

2. As they dialogue and interact with each other, how are the characters in this passage contributing to each other's lives? Contrast the positive traits of some characters with the negative traits of

others. Notice the ways the darkness of some characters accentuates the brilliance of others.

3. In no other genre does our attention so easily drift from God to human beings than in Old Testament narratives. Therefore it is crucial that we constantly ask ourselves, "What does God reveal about himself here?"

Thoughts to guide you:

- Where do you see him confronting people in truth, power, compassion, grace, mercy, judgment, etc.?
- Where do you see him acting in mercy for the guilty, strength for the weak, love for the unlovely and undeserving, provision for the needy, warning for those who are in error, punishment for enemies, and rescue of his people from enemies from whom they cannot rescue themselves?
- Where do you see discipline that turns people back into God's arms and away from unsafe paths?
- Keeping these examples in mind, what evidences of his grace and attributes of his character are predominately on display in this particular passage?

(Continued from previous page)

4. What inconsistency or error in your thinking about God is corrected by seeing his involvement with the characters in this story?

5. What are the prominent concerns and issues in these characters' lives with whom you most identify? Why?

6. Make two lists: one list of the issues involved in this ancient situation, and another list of what might be the contemporary equivalents of those issues.

Ancient Issue	Contemporary Equivalent

QUESTIONS ON 1 SAMUEL 17

The story opens on a battlefield where, in the ongoing war with Israel's greatest enemy—the Philistines—a new tactic is being used. One man, a champion, has been chosen to represent the Philistine army, and he is demanding that the Israelites choose a representative to engage him in battle. The word *champion* in verse 4 can mean *a soldier between the two*, and in this case refers to a man who would fight to the death in representative combat with an opponent from a foreign army.

1. The description of Goliath's armor, which makes him appear invincible, is the longest description of military attire in the entire Old Testament. What effect does his appearance and speech have on the Israelite army?

2. Why do you think Saul does not go out to fight Goliath even though he is the king and official representative of God and the people, not to mention the "giant" of Israel?

3. David speaks for the first time in verse 26. With his first words he articulates a worldview that is the antithesis of the Israelites' thinking. What, in David's theology, should make all the difference in the Israelites' behavior? What should be the starting point in their analysis of the situation?

In what situation in your life do others' external advantages dominate your evaluation? What is your starting point in every evaluation of every situation?

4. List all the ways in this account in which David and his credentials are disdained by men and considered insignificant in their eyes.

How does this illustrate the teaching of 1 Corinthians 1:25–29?

5. David goes out to fight Goliath with some audacious words in verses 45–47. What point does he make about Goliath's impressive armor and weapons?

6. For all true Israelites, armed conflict was fundamentally a religious event, forces under Satan's control coming against God's true people. What truth does David know is always to be the ultimate revelatory goal of a military victory for Israel? (See Joshua 2:10–11; Psalm 18:29–49.)

7. Walter Brueggemann says, "The purpose of David's victory is not simply to save Israel or to defeat the Philistines. The purpose is the glorification of Yahweh in the eyes of the world."[1] What does David want both the Israelite army and Goliath to know about Yahweh (vv. 26, 37, 45, 47)?

1. Walter Brueggemann, *First and Second Samuel* (Louisville: John Knox Press, 1990), 132.

8. The story of David and Goliath is included in the story of David's life to point forward to the day when the Lord sent another anointed hero to fight on behalf of his people who were faced with insurmountable odds and unable to rescue themselves. He too was despised and disdained by men as he, the shepherd warrior, fought to the death as the representative of his people to accomplish the victory over sin and death. Because of his victory God's people are enabled to go forth, trusting God to defeat all the powers arrayed against the living God and his purposes, no matter how great the enemy appears to be. Read John 12:30–32. Even though he has been defeated by Christ at the cross, in what ways does Satan, the "ruler of this world" (John 12:31), still hold sway today to intimidate God's people as Goliath did?

Read Ephesians 6:13–18 and meditate on the great resources God has given us with which to fight as his strength is made perfect in our weakness. What steps will you take this week to deepen your trust in God by using this armor instead of human methods and manipulations?

9. Read verses 55–58. There are many opinions on why it seems Saul does not know who David is. It is David himself who identifies his family to Saul as he proclaims himself to be the son of Jesse, the Bethlehemite. Read Matthew 1:1–6, the beginning of the genealogy of Jesus Christ, to see how God traces the roots of David's participation in the great story of redemption. Now read Ruth 1:1–18; 4:13–22. How did God providentially care for the young woman who brought forth the line of David and ultimately of the Messiah?

What hope does it give you in your own circumstances to know that there is no difficulty that can halt God's purposes to redeem and work in your life for his kingdom's sake?

CONFLICT AND RESOLUTION

1. Where in this story do you see God's people recognizing what their sin deserves, seeing their need of grace, and desperately longing for a divine solution and new life?

2. How do you see the breaking in of the glorious good news of God's provision of the removal of our sin and guilt through the perfect substitute of Jesus Christ's death and resurrection?

APPLICATION

We study Old Testament narratives and all Scripture on a spiritual battlefield. We are constantly pulled back and forth between sinful and righteous living, between self-effort and humble dependence on Christ in us. After studying this passage, ask God to cause you to see with heightened sensitivity what the Holy Spirit wants you to implement in your own life. The application questions we will answer bring us to the "so what?" question. *Why is this passage here? What does God want me to learn/change about me?*

1. What are the ways in which submission to God has taken place in this passage? Where in your own life does it need to take place?

2. What are the ways in which the flesh (selfish desires, manipulation, etc.) has won out in this passage, and how is that showing up in your own life as a need for repentance?

3. Think about how relationship to God has been broken in this passage (due to sin, immaturity, doubt, trial, suffering, etc.). In view of the events in this passage, in what ways does Christ's victory over temptation, sin, and death bring hope, joy, and strength to your walk of faith today?

4. Where in your life will you look for God's gracious provision for your need, forgiveness for your sin, strength in your weakness, discipline or correction as you have seen it here in these lives?

5. What are the truths about God and his rule that you have learned that cause you to rejoice and trust him more?

CONFLICT AND RESOLUTION

1. Where in this story do you see God's people recognizing what their sin deserves, seeing their need of grace, and desperately longing for a divine solution and new life?

2. How do you see the breaking in of the glorious good news of God's provision of the removal of our sin and guilt through the perfect substitute of Jesus Christ's death and resurrection?

APPLICATION

We study Old Testament narratives and all Scripture on a spiritual battlefield. We are constantly pulled back and forth between sinful and righteous living, between self-effort and humble dependence on Christ in us. After studying this passage, ask God to cause you to see with heightened sensitivity what the Holy Spirit wants you to implement in your own life. The application questions we will answer bring us to the "so what?" question. *Why is this passage here? What does God want me to learn/change about me?*

1. What are the ways in which submission to God has taken place in this passage? Where in your own life does it need to take place?

2. What are the ways in which the flesh (selfish desires, manipulation, etc.) has won out in this passage, and how is that showing up in your own life as a need for repentance?

3. Think about how relationship to God has been broken in this passage (due to sin, immaturity, doubt, trial, suffering, etc.). In view of the events in this passage, in what ways does Christ's victory over temptation, sin, and death bring hope, joy, and strength to your walk of faith today?

4. Where in your life will you look for God's gracious provision for your need, forgiveness for your sin, strength in your weakness, discipline or correction as you have seen it here in these lives?

5. What are the truths about God and his rule that you have learned that cause you to rejoice and trust him more?

6. Finally, always in application, ask yourself these three questions:

- *What* does God require of me as a result of having learned the truths of this passage?

- *Where* in my life do I need to do it? What specific area of my life needs this implementation?

- *Why* and *how* can I do it? We will answer this one together. The power of the resurrected, ascended Lord Jesus Christ indwells his people. It is by him, through him, and for him that you are enabled to obey. The compulsion of grace causes us to want to obey and grow in holiness. He sets us apart to holiness when he saves us by a powerful working of his Spirit in our lives that enables us to live for him. The Westminster Confession, chapter 16, says, "Good works done in obedience to God's commandments are the fruits and evidences of a true and lively faith, but a Christian's ability to do good works is not at all of themselves but wholly of the Spirit of Christ."

We must recognize in some way every passage points not only to our need of redemption, but also to God's provision of our redemption, including his enabling, powerful Holy Spirit. The Bible is not a self-help book. "Apart from me you can do nothing," Jesus said (John 15:5).

Pray that the Holy Spirit will cause us to consider what to fight, where to fight, why to fight, and how to fight anything that comes against that growth in holiness.

1 Samuel 24–26

THESE CHAPTERS SHOW a contrast in David's mode of behavior when dealing with different difficult situations. As he continues to make his way in the wilderness, the opportunity presents itself several times for him to take matters into his own hands. For the first time in David's story, he is seen acting in an unethical way. God will not let the reader make a hero of David. The Bible is not about David's redemptive actions. It is about God's mighty saving acts on behalf of his sinful people, including David. Read carefully to see the ways in which God saves David in each situation. Each of the three stories is an account of God's testing of David so that David can know with certainty that Yahweh can be trusted to be his Vindicator and his Savior.

MEDITATION AND DISCOVERY

1. Read the entire passage and, as you read, become aware of the details of the settings, situations, and crises of peoples' lives. Circle or write down repeated words that will highlight the narrator's emphasis. Circle or write down contrasting words. Circle or write down scene-changing words.

2. Write down questions that come to mind that you expect or hope will be answered as you study. These might include but are certainly not limited to:

    • What does this particular thing mean?
    • Where is this happening?
    • Why are they doing this particular thing?
    • What surprises you in the story?

    Good interpretation involves asking many questions of the text!

6. Finally, always in application, ask yourself these three questions:

- *What* does God require of me as a result of having learned the truths of this passage?

- *Where* in my life do I need to do it? What specific area of my life needs this implementation?

- *Why* and *how* can I do it? We will answer this one together. The power of the resurrected, ascended Lord Jesus Christ indwells his people. It is by him, through him, and for him that you are enabled to obey. The compulsion of grace causes us to want to obey and grow in holiness. He sets us apart to holiness when he saves us by a powerful working of his Spirit in our lives that enables us to live for him. The Westminster Confession, chapter 16, says, "Good works done in obedience to God's commandments are the fruits and evidences of a true and lively faith, but a Christian's ability to do good works is not at all of themselves but wholly of the Spirit of Christ."

205

In what ways does David transcend the bad memories and focus on what he wants Israel to remember about Saul?

3. David speaks of the public grief that all Israel should share, but at the end his inconsolable thoughts are about Jonathan alone, his most trusted confidant and companion, the one whom David loved as he loved himself. What does it mean to love someone as you love yourself? How is this even possible? (See Philippians 1:3–9; 2:1–8; Ephesians 4:1–6.)

Chapter 2

David consults the Lord for his next step and is directed to Hebron, a city of Judah, David's ancestral tribe. This city looms large in the memories of God's covenant family since many of David's ancestors are buried there. Abraham, Sarah, Isaac, Rebekah, Jacob, and Leah all share this common resting place. It becomes David's first seat of power and is where he is first publicly anointed, although only by the Judahite elders. Although it is a far cry from the rule of all Israel, as Dale Ralph Davis says, it is "here for the first time [that] Yahweh's chosen king visibly rules on earth."[2]

4. We have seen in previous lessons that God promised the patriarch Abraham that kings would come from his body. By the time of his grandson Jacob's deathbed prophecies, how has the promise been narrowed down and specified? (See Genesis 49:8–12.)

Although it will be seven years before this promise will come to fruition in David's life, this royal oracle will not ultimately fail. What is it we are to remember when our little portion of the kingdom seems insignificant and ineffective and the world is in chaos? (See Ephesians 1:19–22.)

What things in your life tend to distract you from that truth?

2. Davis, *2 Samuel*, 28.

5. Because David is a Judahite, the elders of Judah are the most likely to welcome him as king. What action has he already taken that gives them reasons for readily accepting him? (See 1 Samuel 30:26–31.)

   What other winsome action does he take in verses 5–6 to ensure his acceptance with loyal supporters of Saul in Jabesh-gilead as the kingdom is expanded?

   How do David's words to them, which make promises about the character of his reign, anticipate the words of his great descendant's invitation to come under his lordship? (See Matthew 11:28–30.)

6. During this time, the war between the house of Saul and the house of David begins. Saul's one remaining son, Ish-bosheth, is named king over the remaining tribes of Israel. But the

real power behind the throne is Abner, the commander of Saul's armies.

The rest of the chapter is the bizarre and bloody story of the conflict between the two "kingdoms" as played out by Saul's men under Abner's command and David's men under Joab's command. During a standoff at the pool of Gibeon, Abner suggests a gladiator-like tournament, and twenty-four young men die in gruesome one-on-one combat. As the confrontation escalates, David's nephew Asahel dies at the hand of Abner, making Abner the target of Joab. What repeated word does the narrator use in verses 26–27 to characterize this division?

What, in David's own words, is important to God in this new kingdom? (See Psalm 133:1.)

Chapter 3

7. Unfortunately David's words from Psalm 133 never characterize his own family, as the rest of 2 Samuel demonstrates. In verses 1–5, what already obvious issue is going to be a problem in David's family?

8. Abner eventually throws his loyalty to David and enters into negotiations with him, promising to deliver the northern tribes. David's first condition is that he get his wife Michal back. The scene is heartbreaking as her grief-stricken current husband follows her to Hebron. On whom should the blame be laid for this sad situation? (See 1 Samuel 25:44.)

Why do you think David insists on getting Michal back now that he has been anointed king over Judah?

What other actions does the politically savvy Abner take to ensure his partnership with David?

What phrase is repeated three times in verses 21–23 to emphasize David's true feelings regarding this new relationship with Saul's former right-hand man?

9. After Joab's murder of Abner, a shocked David goes to great lengths to disassociate himself from any guilt. What are the

demonstrative ways in which he disavows all responsibility for Abner's death?

How do the people of Israel respond?

Chapter 4

10. The bloodshed continues as opportunists of all stripes try to get into the good graces of the man who is clearly going to be the king of all Israel. When the sons of Rimmon murder Ish-bosheth in his bed and bring his head to David as a trophy, their misguided notion is that they have been useful in finally ridding David of his enemies, Saul's family. Where is David's properly placed gratitude for deliverance?

11. With the gory execution of these two men, David is once again forced to take extreme measures to address injustice. David knows that he will be king. What is the message he continues to send publicly about justice in God's kingdom (vv. 9–11)? Read Revelation 11:16–18. What is the theme of this song of the consummated kingdom of God to which David's actions point?

12. David's kingship pointed God's people forward in hope to a day when David's descendent would come and establish his throne of justice and holiness forever. Read carefully and meditate on Isaiah 9:6–7. Hundreds of years after David, Isaiah boldly proclaims the magnificence of the coming son of David. But he does more than just proclaim it—he makes it personal. He says, "To *us* a son is given." What are the ways in which you personally have been the blessed recipient of the gift of this son as he is described in Isaiah 9? For example, when have you known him as Wonderful Counselor, Prince of Peace, etc.?

CONFLICT AND RESOLUTION

1. Where in this story do you see God's people recognizing what their sin deserves, seeing their need of grace, and desperately longing for a divine solution and new life?

2. How do you see the breaking in of the glorious good news of God's provision of the removal of our sin and guilt through the perfect substitute of Jesus Christ's death and resurrection?

APPLICATION

We study Old Testament narratives and all Scripture on a spiritual battlefield. We are constantly pulled back and forth between sinful and righteous living, between self-effort and humble dependence on Christ in us. After studying this passage, ask God to cause you to see with heightened sensitivity what the Holy Spirit wants you to implement in your own life. The application questions we will answer bring us to the "so what?" question. *Why is this passage here? What does God want me to learn/change about me?*

1. What are the ways in which submission to God has taken place in this passage? Where in your own life does it need to take place?

2. What are the ways in which the flesh (selfish desires, manipulation, etc.) has won out in this passage, and how is that showing up in your own life as a need for repentance?

3. Think about how relationship to God has been broken in this passage (due to sin, immaturity, doubt, trial, suffering, etc.). In view of the events in this passage, in what ways does Christ's victory over temptation, sin, and death bring hope, joy, and strength to your walk of faith today?

4. Where in your life will you look for God's gracious provision for your need, forgiveness for your sin, strength in your weakness, discipline or correction as you have seen it here in these lives?

5. What are the truths about God and his rule that you have learned that cause you to rejoice and trust him more?

6. Finally, always in application, ask yourself these three questions:

- *What* does God require of me as a result of having learned the truths of this passage?

- *Where* in my life do I need to do it? What specific area of my life needs this implementation?

- *Why* and *how* can I do it? We will answer this one together. The power of the resurrected, ascended Lord Jesus Christ indwells his people. It is by him, through him, and for him that you are enabled to obey. The compulsion of grace causes us to want to obey and grow in holiness. He sets us apart to holiness when he saves us by a powerful working of his Spirit in our lives that enables us to live for him. The Westminster Confession, chapter 16, says, "Good works done in obedience to God's commandments are the fruits and evidences of a true and lively faith, but a Christian's ability to do good works is not at all of themselves but wholly of the Spirit of Christ."

We must recognize in some way every passage points not only to our need of redemption, but also to God's provision of our redemption, including his enabling, powerful Holy Spirit. The Bible is not a self-help book. "Apart from me you can do nothing," Jesus said (John 15:5).

Pray that the Holy Spirit will cause us to consider what to fight, where to fight, why to fight, and how to fight anything that comes against that growth in holiness.

LESSON 14

2 Samuel 5–6

AFTER A BLOODY CIVIL WAR, David becomes king over all Israel. What was once a disorganized, warring collection of tribes becomes a true theocratic nation unified under the king "after God's own heart." Under the rule of David, Israel sees the fulfillment of the promises made to Abraham in ways that bring her to the apex of her history thus far. This passage highlights key events in David's reign and demonstrates what should always be characteristic of God's people as they live in unity under God's rule.

MEDITATION AND DISCOVERY

1. Read the entire passage and, as you read, become aware of the details of the settings, situations, and crises of peoples' lives. Circle or write down repeated words that will highlight the narrator's emphasis. Circle or write down contrasting words. Circle or write down scene-changing words.

2. Write down questions that come to mind that you expect or hope will be answered as you study. These might include but are certainly not limited to:

   • What does this particular thing mean?
   • Where is this happening?
   • Why are they doing this particular thing?
   • What surprises you in the story?

   Good interpretation involves asking many questions of the text!

3. What stories precede and follow this passage, and what light do these "next-door neighbors" shed on the passage? Determine how this particular passage fits into the central idea of all 1 and 2 Samuel. Expand the context to the whole Bible. How does the passage fit into the whole story of Scripture? What was the author's intent, and what would the original audience have understood?

4. After reading and rereading the passage, what do you think is the main idea or theme of this particular passage?

3. Think about how relationship to God has been broken in this passage (due to sin, immaturity, doubt, trial, suffering, etc.). In view of the events in this passage, in what ways does Christ's victory over temptation, sin, and death bring hope, joy, and strength to your walk of faith today?

4. Where in your life will you look for God's gracious provision for your need, forgiveness for your sin, strength in your weakness, discipline or correction as you have seen it here in these lives?

5. What are the truths about God and his rule that you have learned that cause you to rejoice and trust him more?

6. Finally, always in application, ask yourself these three questions:

- *What* does God require of me as a result of having learned the truths of this passage?

- *Where* in my life do I need to do it? What specific area of my life needs this implementation?

- *Why* and *how* can I do it? We will answer this one together. The power of the resurrected, ascended Lord Jesus Christ indwells his people. It is by him, through him, and for him that you are enabled to obey. The compulsion of grace causes us to want to obey and grow in holiness. He sets us apart to holiness when he saves us by a powerful working of his Spirit in our lives that enables us to live for him. The Westminster Confession, chapter 16, says, "Good works done in obedience to God's commandments are the fruits and evidences of a true and lively faith, but a Christian's ability to do good works is not at all of themselves but wholly of the Spirit of Christ."

We must recognize in some way every passage points not only to our need of redemption, but also to God's provision of our redemption, including his enabling, powerful Holy Spirit. The Bible is not a self-help book. "Apart from me you can do nothing," Jesus said (John 15:5).

Pray that the Holy Spirit will cause us to consider what to fight, where to fight, why to fight, and how to fight anything that comes against that growth in holiness.

LESSON 15

2 Samuel 7-8

IN THIS PASSAGE we come to God's all-important covenant with David. There is a trajectory in the covenants God makes with his people in the Old Testament. Each covenant moves the redemptive story along. Each one builds on the one that comes before it and forms a driving force for the one to come. It is as if, with each new covenant, relationship with God is deepened and changed so that the people of God can no longer live as they had before. With each new covenant there is a new understanding of God and what he is doing to redeem his people. There is new responsibility and new promise and new revelation. The seed of the woman who will crush the serpent's head is now revealed to be a royal seed. Promises are fulfilled and new ones made with each new covenant. The covenant relationship of God with his people is typified by promises. But the covenants are always reciprocal. David will fail to carry out royal covenant responsibilities placed on him, and his failures will be a constant reminder of the overwhelming need for the King who will come on his people's behalf and rule faithfully.

David has been chosen, anointed, crowned, loved, settled, and given victories. But in the passage before us, we come to the pinnacle of God's grace to him. As we continue to read the story of David's life and see how it is punctuated by sin and failure, we must, as David did, go back again and again to these promises. They remind

David until the end of his life that Yahweh has perfectly ordered and planned David's life for the glory of Yahweh and the good of his people and that he is faithful to carry out his covenant promises. Just as David and generations after him have been, we are reminded that the promises to which we cling in faith are as sure as the everlasting God who made them and that they will never falter nor fail.

MEDITATION AND DISCOVERY

1. Read the entire passage and, as you read, become aware of the details of the settings, situations, and crises of peoples' lives. Circle or write down repeated words that will highlight the narrator's emphasis. Circle or write down contrasting words. Circle or write down scene-changing words.

2. Write down questions that come to mind that you expect or hope will be answered as you study. These might include but are certainly not limited to:

   • What does this particular thing mean?
   • Where is this happening?
   • Why are they doing this particular thing?
   • What surprises you in the story?

   Good interpretation involves asking many questions of the text!

3. What stories precede and follow this passage, and what light do these "next-door neighbors" shed on the passage? Determine how this particular passage fits into the central idea of all 1 and 2 Samuel. Expand the context to the whole Bible. How does the passage fit into the whole story of Scripture? What was the author's intent, and what would the original audience have understood?

4. After reading and rereading the passage, what do you think is the main idea or theme of this particular passage?

CHARACTERIZATION AND SCENES

1. Make a list of characters and identify habits, desires, emotions, overt actions, and speech of each that give clues to their relationship to God and what is in their hearts. What is God's evaluation of their conduct and character?

2. As they dialogue and interact with each other, how are the characters in this passage contributing to each other's lives? Contrast the positive traits of some characters with the negative traits of

others. Notice the ways the darkness of some characters accentuates the brilliance of others.

3. In no other genre does our attention so easily drift from God to human beings than in Old Testament narratives. Therefore it is crucial that we constantly ask ourselves, "What does God reveal about himself here?"

Thoughts to guide you:

- Where do you see him confronting people in truth, power, compassion, grace, mercy, judgment, etc.?
- Where do you see him acting in mercy for the guilty, strength for the weak, love for the unlovely and undeserving, provision for the needy, warning for those who are in error, punishment for enemies, and rescue of his people from enemies from whom they cannot rescue themselves?
- Where do you see discipline that turns people back into God's arms and away from unsafe paths?
- Keeping these examples in mind, what evidences of his grace and attributes of his character are predominately on display in this particular passage?

4. What inconsistency or error in your thinking about God is corrected by seeing his involvement with the characters in this story?

5. What are the prominent concerns and issues in these characters' lives with whom you most identify? Why?

CONFLICT AND RESOLUTION

1. Where in this story do you see God's people recognizing what their sin deserves, seeing their need of grace, and desperately longing for a divine solution and new life?

2. How do you see the breaking in of the glorious good news of God's provision of the removal of our sin and guilt through the perfect substitute of Jesus Christ's death and resurrection?

APPLICATION

We study Old Testament narratives and all Scripture on a spiritual battlefield. We are constantly pulled back and forth between sinful and righteous living, between self-effort and humble dependence on Christ in us. After studying this passage, ask God to cause you to see with heightened sensitivity what the Holy Spirit wants you to implement in your own life. The application questions we will answer bring us to the "so what?" question. *Why is this passage here? What does God want me to learn/change about me?*

1. What are the ways in which submission to God has taken place in this passage? Where in your own life does it need to take place?

2. What are the ways in which the flesh (selfish desires, manipulation, etc.) has won out in this passage, and how is that showing up in your own life as a need for repentance?

3. Think about how relationship to God has been broken in this passage (due to sin, immaturity, doubt, trial, suffering, etc.). In view of the events in this passage, in what ways does Christ's victory over temptation, sin, and death bring hope, joy, and strength to your walk of faith today?

4. Where in your life will you look for God's gracious provision for your need, forgiveness for your sin, strength in your weakness, discipline or correction as you have seen it here in these lives?

5. What are the truths about God and his rule that you have learned that cause you to rejoice and trust him more?

311

6. Finally, always in application, ask yourself these three questions:

- *What* does God require of me as a result of having learned the truths of this passage?

- *Where* in my life do I need to do it? What specific area of my life needs this implementation?

- *Why* and *how* can I do it? We will answer this one together. The power of the resurrected, ascended Lord Jesus Christ indwells his people. It is by him, through him, and for him that you are enabled to obey. The compulsion of grace causes us to want to obey and grow in holiness. He sets us apart to holiness when he saves us by a powerful working of his Spirit in our lives that enables us to live for him. The Westminster Confession, chapter 16, says, "Good works done in obedience to God's commandments are the fruits and evidences of a true and lively faith, but a Christian's ability to do good works is not at all of themselves but wholly of the Spirit of Christ."

We must recognize in some way every passage points not only to our need of redemption, but also to God's provision of our redemption, including his enabling, powerful Holy Spirit. The Bible is not a self-help book. "Apart from me you can do nothing," Jesus said (John 15:5).

Pray that the Holy Spirit will cause us to consider what to fight, where to fight, why to fight, and how to fight anything that comes against that growth in holiness.

LESSON 17

2 Samuel 11–12

THESE TWO CHAPTERS tell one single story, the pivotal story that sets the course of events for the rest of 2 Samuel and all of 1 and 2 Kings. The narrative of David's relationship with Yahweh up to this point has been one of unbroken fellowship, covenant fidelity, and unlimited blessings. But now we come to the point at which the king who has known nothing but the blessings of God breaks fellowship with God in such an abhorrent way that he comes under God's severe discipline. The sins David commits will have a devastating effect on his family and the nation of Israel. This is a story that is almost more than we can bear to read about David, because it so clearly shows us how easily God's own people can rebel against him. And yet in his grace our God has told us the story so that we can see the heinousness of sin through his eyes and marvel at the cleansing and forgiveness that only he can provide.

MEDITATION AND DISCOVERY

1. Read the entire passage and, as you read, become aware of the details of the settings, situations, and crises of peoples' lives. Circle or write down repeated words that will highlight the narrator's emphasis. Circle or write down contrasting words. Circle or write down scene-changing words.

2. Write down questions that come to mind that you expect or hope will be answered as you study. These might include but are certainly not limited to:

   • What does this particular thing mean?
   • Where is this happening?
   • Why are they doing this particular thing?
   • What surprises you in the story?

   Good interpretation involves asking many questions of the text!

3. What stories precede and follow this passage, and what light do these "next-door neighbors" shed on the passage? Determine how this particular passage fits into the central idea of all 1 and 2 Samuel. Expand the context to the whole Bible. How does the passage fit into the whole story of Scripture? What was the author's intent, and what would the original audience have understood?

4. After reading and rereading the passage, what do you think is the main idea or theme of this particular passage?

CHARACTERIZATION AND SCENES

1. Make a list of characters and identify habits, desires, emotions, overt actions, and speech of each that give clues to their relationship to God and what is in their hearts. What is God's evaluation of their conduct and character?

2. As they dialogue and interact with each other, how are the characters in this passage contributing to each other's lives? Contrast the positive traits of some characters with the negative traits of

others. Notice the ways the darkness of some characters accentuates the brilliance of others.

3. In no other genre does our attention so easily drift from God to human beings than in Old Testament narratives. Therefore it is crucial that we constantly ask ourselves, "What does God reveal about himself here?"

Thoughts to guide you:

- Where do you see him confronting people in truth, power, compassion, grace, mercy, judgment, etc.?
- Where do you see him acting in mercy for the guilty, strength for the weak, love for the unlovely and undeserving, provision for the needy, warning for those who are in error, punishment for enemies, and rescue of his people from enemies from whom they cannot rescue themselves?
- Where do you see discipline that turns people back into God's arms and away from unsafe paths?
- Keeping these examples in mind, what evidences of his grace and attributes of his character are predominately on display in this particular passage?

319

(Continued from previous page)

4. What inconsistency or error in your thinking about God is corrected by seeing his involvement with the characters in this story?

5. What are the prominent concerns and issues in these characters' lives with whom you most identify? Why?

6. Make two lists: one list of the issues involved in this ancient situation, and another list of what might be the contemporary equivalents of those issues.

Ancient Issue	Contemporary Equivalent

QUESTIONS ON 2 SAMUEL 11–12

Chapter 11

1. When the story opens, there is still a long and difficult war going on with the Ammonites. In this first scene, how does the narrator alert the reader from the outset that already something is abnormal?

   What might have been the mental attitude of David in the spring of this new "war year" against the Ammonites? Consider 2 Samuel 5:25; 8:6–8, 13–14; 10:18–19.

2. From the beginning the responsibility for the sins is placed completely and squarely on David alone. Trace the progression of David's sin by listing the verbs in verses 2–4.

3. Once Bathsheba sends word to David that she is pregnant, he plots a cover-up. After Uriah is sent for and begins to interact with David, everything about David's actions reveals him to be in complete contrast to Uriah. We are told three times that Uriah does not go home. What is the amazing reason this man, who is not a member of Israel's covenant community, gives for not enjoying his leave from duty?

What is the irony of Uriah saying this to the covenant king?

4. When all the schemes of his first cover-up fail, David sends Uriah's death warrant to Joab via Uriah's own hand! David's second plot works quickly because of Joab's cooperation, but there are hints of Joab's disgust. Why do you think Joab in his instructions to the messenger brings up a very old incident of a death caused by a woman?

others. Notice the ways the darkness of some characters accentuates the brilliance of others.

3. In no other genre does our attention so easily drift from God to human beings than in Old Testament narratives. Therefore it is crucial that we constantly ask ourselves, "What does God reveal about himself here?"

Thoughts to guide you:

- Where do you see him confronting people in truth, power, compassion, grace, mercy, judgment, etc.?
- Where do you see him acting in mercy for the guilty, strength for the weak, love for the unlovely and undeserving, provision for the needy, warning for those who are in error, punishment for enemies, and rescue of his people from enemies from whom they cannot rescue themselves?
- Where do you see discipline that turns people back into God's arms and away from unsafe paths?
- Keeping these examples in mind, what evidences of his grace and attributes of his character are predominately on display in this particular passage?

(Continued from previous page)

4. What inconsistency or error in your thinking about God is corrected by seeing his involvement with the characters in this story?

5. What are the prominent concerns and issues in these characters' lives with whom you most identify? Why?

6. Make two lists: one list of the issues involved in this ancient situation, and another list of what might be the contemporary equivalents of those issues.

Ancient Issue	Contemporary Equivalent

QUESTIONS ON 2 SAMUEL 15-17

Chapter 15

1. According to verses 1–6, how does Absalom go about stealing the hearts of the people of Israel?

   What contrast is he trying to draw between himself and his father in the people's minds?

2. Where do we see these tactics on the world stage today, and what can we learn here about their effects on people?

When it comes to political discussions, what differences do you hear between people with a biblical worldview and those who have little or no knowledge of the Bible?

What difference does it make to your level of anxiety and fearfulness when every aspect of your view of world affairs is shaped and informed by Scripture?

3. After Absalom gets to Hebron, he activates his strategy to seize the throne. When David hears that the conspiracy is successful, he makes plans to evacuate Jerusalem with those loyal to him, probably in an effort to avoid bloodshed in the "City of Peace." In a poignant scene, he pauses at the last house before leaving the city to watch his supporters, many of whom are non-Israelites,

pass by. How do we see the graciousness of David in his dealings with Ittai the Gittite?

What is Ittai's response, and what is the evidence in verse 22 that Ittai is truly entrusting everything to his king and his king's God?

Read Luke 14:15–28. According to that passage, what are some of the aspects of following the true King Jesus that are being anticipated in this ancient scene in 2 Samuel 15:18–23 involving King David and Ittai the Gittite?

4. What can we learn about David's assessment of his usefulness to God from his decision regarding the ark of God?

What can we learn from this about how freeing true faith in God is?

Although David is in complete submission to God's will, how does he then demonstrate that confidence in God's sovereignty does not mean we sit passively by and do nothing?

5. Trace the similarities between the betrayed King David in 2 Samuel 15:30–31 and the true King Jesus when he was betrayed, as described in the following verses.

• Luke 22:39

• Luke 23:27

According to Luke 23:28–30, for whom should all conspirators against the Lord's anointed be mourning?

6. David receives the devastating news that his trusted counselor, Ahithophel, has betrayed him. Why might Ahithophel have sided with Absalom rather than staying with David? Look at 2 Samuel 11:3 and 2 Samuel 23:34 for a probable answer.

Chapter 16

7. As David proceeds on his flight from the coup, he has two painful encounters with members of Saul's tribe. Ziba attempts to curry favor with the king with lies about Mephibosheth, and Shimei curses the king while physically assaulting him. Considering the events of the day, why do you think David might have been so quick to believe Ziba's lies? (See also 2 Samuel 17:1–2a.)

In the midst of the emotional, physical, and psychological pain of fleeing his own son, David writes Psalm 3. Read John 13:21–38; 19:1–3. What are the ways in which King David's suffering prefigures Christ's suffering among his own people?

8. Scholars throughout the ages have agreed that the encounter between Hushai and Absalom in verses 16–18 is one of the most irony-filled scenes in this passage, with Hushai speaking in double meanings. If this is true, what is he really saying each time he speaks to Absalom?

9. How is Nathan's prophecy of 2 Samuel 12:11–12, that David will reap what he has sown, vividly fulfilled in verses 20–22?

In observing this incredibly immoral scene, what can we also learn about what God is saying in regard to this ancient Eastern family system of concubines that had infiltrated his monarchy?

Consider and write down some practices of the present-day culture that, because we do not think of them as sinful, may infiltrate our own family life.

Chapter 17

10. Ahithophel, sensing that he has now officially handed over the kingdom to Absalom, puts forth his plan to kill David. As effective as his plan would be for Absalom's purposes, Absalom makes a quick decision to ask Hushai his opinion as well. How does Hushai's creative and completely pro-David plan appeal to Absalom's immense ego and ambition?

Why does Absalom choose Hushai's plan over Ahithophel's?

11. At this point no one in the story knows why Hushai's plan has
    been chosen except you, the reader. Not only does Hushai not
    know *why*, he does not know *if* his plan was chosen. David's
    undercover network quickly begins to work out its actions in
    secret to accomplish what God has ordained, "to bring harm
    upon Absalom" (v. 14). Even the acts of treason against David
    are carried out under God's direction of and ultimate destination
    for his anointed king. How does all this anticipate what Peter
    explains happened to Jesus in Acts 2:22–24?

12. Read Matthew 16:15–18. What must we who are members of
    his church know about King Jesus and those who are his?

How does knowing God's ultimate purposes give you comfort and perspective in your daily life?

13. This passage ends not with David's enemies and traitors, but with friends and supporters. They stand with Yahweh's chosen king and meet the practical needs of David's exiled government. We do not know when David wrote Psalm 23, which is so well known and beloved, but it could have easily been within this time frame. Read Psalm 23 and jot down verses that might correspond to what David is actually experiencing at this particular time and what he knows to be true about God.

David has dealt in kindness and justice with those who follow him as he leads them into the unknown:

David knows that this might be his last night on earth if Ahithophel's plan succeeds:

David knows that he is Yahweh's anointed king:

David is provided with life-sustaining food in the midst of advancing troops:

David has been given a promise by Yahweh that his house and kingdom will be established forever:

Where do you need to recognize the hand of the Lord, your Shepherd, intervening on your behalf with his gracious provisions in the midst of bad situations?

CONFLICT AND RESOLUTION

1. Where in this story do you see God's people recognizing what their sin deserves, seeing their need of grace, and desperately longing for a divine solution and new life?

2. How do you see the breaking in of the glorious good news of God's provision of the removal of our sin and guilt through the perfect substitute of Jesus Christ's death and resurrection?

APPLICATION

We study Old Testament narratives and all Scripture on a spiritual battlefield. We are constantly pulled back and forth between sinful and righteous living, between self-effort and humble dependence on Christ in us. After studying this passage, ask God to cause you to see with heightened sensitivity what the Holy Spirit wants you to implement in your own life. The application questions we will answer bring us to the "so what?" question. *Why is this passage here? What does God want me to learn/change about me?*

1. What are the ways in which submission to God has taken place in this passage? Where in your own life does it need to take place?

2. What are the ways in which the flesh (selfish desires, manipulation, etc.) has won out in this passage, and how is that showing up in your own life as a need for repentance?

others. Notice the ways the darkness of some characters accentuates the brilliance of others.

3. In no other genre does our attention so easily drift from God to human beings than in Old Testament narratives. Therefore it is crucial that we constantly ask ourselves, "What does God reveal about himself here?"

Thoughts to guide you:

- Where do you see him confronting people in truth, power, compassion, grace, mercy, judgment, etc.?
- Where do you see him acting in mercy for the guilty, strength for the weak, love for the unlovely and undeserving, provision for the needy, warning for those who are in error, punishment for enemies, and rescue of his people from enemies from whom they cannot rescue themselves?
- Where do you see discipline that turns people back into God's arms and away from unsafe paths?
- Keeping these examples in mind, what evidences of his grace and attributes of his character are predominately on display in this particular passage?

405

(Continued from previous page)

4. What inconsistency or error in your thinking about God is corrected by seeing his involvement with the characters in this story?

5. What are the prominent concerns and issues in these characters' lives with whom you most identify? Why?

6. Make two lists: one list of the issues involved in this ancient situation, and another list of what might be the contemporary equivalents of those issues.

ANCIENT ISSUE	CONTEMPORARY EQUIVALENT

QUESTIONS ON 2 SAMUEL 21-22

Chapter 21

1. In order to understand this strange story, we must look back at the original incident. Read Joshua 9:3–20 to see the deception of the Gibeonites that caused the original oath for their protection to be made. Fast-forward to the reign of King Saul, Yahweh's representative, when they are killed in spite of the oath made in Yahweh's name to protect them. Now that the problem has been dumped in David's lap and identified by God, what is David asked to do to appease the Gibeonites?

2. How do we see in verse 3 that it is the Lord's name and reputation that have been violated?

3. The story is gruesome and completely baffling to the contemporary Western mind. It is often said that the God of the Old Testament

is harsh and full of wrath, but Jesus Christ, the God of the New Testament, is gentle, meek, and merciful. What lack of understanding of the Lord does this reveal? (See Revelation 19:11–21.)

4. As difficult as this passage is, it reveals several important things about the wrath of God against those who break covenant with him. Where in this story do you see

- the revelation of his wrath?

- the self-control of his wrath?

- the reason for his wrath?

- the deliverance from his wrath?

Preface

Je cherche à déchiffrer le plus indéchiffrable
des peuples, le plus moral, le moins familial,
le plus mobile, le plus adapté, le plus franc et
le plus hypocrite. Où est le principe?
                                    Elie Halévy[1]

To many people an enterprise such as the writing of this book would
appear to present an impossible challenge. No one is more aware of this
than the author. By its content and by its intent the book purports not
only to describe the evolution of modern English society in its broad
patterns, but to provide a critical assessment of this evolution, in order to
interpret and explain the history of the nation. An arduous task in any
circumstances, but especially so for a foreigner, for it must seem utterly
presumptuous.

The social make-up, the attitudes and behaviour, the psychology of the
English people during these one hundred and twenty-five years provide
such a tangle of data, fleeting and contradictory at the same time, that the
task may seem hopeless. As soon as one tries to analyse the true nature of
the islanders, it vanishes; and in contact with it one constantly has the
feeling that it cannot be grasped. This impression has indeed been shared
by all those who have sought to penetrate the nation's secret. Even
Baron von Bülow, when he was Prussian envoy in London, used to
say to his compatriots who asked him his views on the country: 'After
spending three weeks in England, I was quite ready to write a book about

it; after three months I thought the task would be difficult; and now that I've lived here three years, I find it impossible.'[2] About forty years later, the radical novelist Jules Vallès echoed this sentiment when he confessed on his first visit to the English capital: 'After a three weeks' stay in London I became aware that, to be able to talk about England, a stay of ten years would be necessary.'[3]

The British too have felt puzzled when trying to characterize and understand their own civilization. Asking himself in 1940 what constituted the particular nature of the English nation, and how it differed from other nations, George Orwell concluded: 'Yes, there is something distinctive and recognisable in English civilisation. It is a culture as individual as that of Spain. It is somehow bound up with solid breakfasts and gloomy Sundays, smoky towns and winding roads, green fields and red pillar-boxes. It has a flavour of its own.' But such peculiar features, Orwell rightly went on, cannot be properly understood outside the historical setting:

> It is continuous, it stretches into the future and the past, there is something in it that persists as in a living creature. What can the England of 1940 have in common with the England of 1840? But then, what have you in common with the child of five whose photograph your mother keeps on the mantelpiece? Nothing, except that you happen to be the same person. And above all it is *your* civilisation, it is *you*.[4]

So it is easy to understand why foreign observers have often hesitated before launching into mastering the labyrinth without Ariadne's thread – even, and indeed above all, when they have wished to be solicitous and sympathetic to the object of their study. For the more scrupulous they are, the more they feel condemned to look in from outside. Thus Elie Halévy, in the introduction to his great *History of the English People in the Nineteenth Century*, admitted his foolhardiness at once and confessed his fears in these terms:

> Frenchmen, I am undertaking a history of England. I am attempting the study of a people to whom I am foreign alike by birth and by education. Despite copious readings, visits to London and to the provinces, and frequent intercourse with different circles of English society, I have nevertheless been obliged to learn with great difficulty, and in a manner that would seem necessarily artificial, a multitude of things which even an uneducated Englishman knows, so to speak, by instinct. I fully realize all this. Nevertheless I am firmly convinced that the risks I have taken were risks well worth the taking.[5]

Indeed a historian must surmount these obstacles and difficulties. In his own defence Halévy mentioned the 'useful faculty of astonishment' which a foreigner, looking from the outside, preserves towards the subject of his study. It is undeniable that such an approach encourages a critical mind and the will to ask questions and explain. Moreover, following the lead of another clever student of English politics and society, Jacques Bardoux, one can add another argument: 'Distance allows one to observe calmly and to judge dispassionately. Space is as important as time in giving perspective. A channel, when one wants to scrutinise and understand, is as valuable as a century. It ensures, or it ought to ensure, clarity of vision and calmness of judgment.'[6]

For my part, it is in this spirit that I have undertaken this work. It is for the reader to decide how good a job has been done.

Let me now try, at whatever risk, to make a list of the key problems which we have made a point of emphasizing in the pages to come. It will at least be a first step towards clarifying the field of investigation, and a way of tracing out in broad strokes the framework of our study.

(1) The history of England shows a national continuity. A territorial continuity, first of all, thanks to the rampart of the sea, but above all a political continuity. Comparison with all the other great nations of continental Europe is instructive on this point. Why did England escape not only revolutions, bloody violence and attempts at totalitarianism, but also internal upsets, civil discord and drastic changes of regimes and institutions?

(2) In a society of such clear-cut class distinctions, where social mobility has not been as real as some have made out, how has the ruling oligarchy – aristocratic at first, and later bourgeois – succeeded in keeping its influence as well as its prestige, and all this with the full acquiescence of the masses?

(3) How can one explain the fact that the working class – as powerful in numbers as in organization – fought so vigorously and doggedly, and yet so often accepted compromise when its loyalty to the representative system gave it such a key numerical advantage?

(4) How far was power democratized? Who ruled the country a century ago? Who rules today? Exactly how much power did the State have throughout this period? Was it as feeble (at least up to 1914) as has been maintained? How was the link between State, capitalism and the Establishment preserved?

(5) An unusual balance was kept between the individual and the collective, between liberty and constraint, between individualism and the pressure of the consensus. What were the elements which made up this equilibrium? How were the aspirations to individual independence ('the freeborn Englishman') reconciled with a community spirit (itself

reinforced by the pressure of conformity)? In this area, what role was played by religious beliefs?

(6) How did an imperial vocation and the dynamism of an expansionist society settle into the national consciousness? And, when the time came for England to give up her world role, how did she make the change from pride to humility? Under what conditions did the shift take place towards a new model of society limited to a medium-sized island and above all jealous of 'the quality of life'?

(7) What really changed between 1851 and 1975, either in social structure or in the public mind? How did England adapt, by its internal and external development, to the new conditions of the contemporary world – economic, political, intellectual and spiritual? What part was played in this process by religion and the decline of religion, by ideologies and scales of value? And what happened to the consensus of the old days?

Of course this book can only bring partial answers and very modest offerings of interpretation to questions of such wide scope. We would feel well satisfied if the pages that follow helped to open up certain paths of investigation and shed some beams of light on an area that is wrapped in obscurity.

Let us, however, confess to one ambition. I would wish through this work to help get rid of some traditional clichés, to which people refer as if they were gospel. Let us put an end to pseudo-explanations deriving from the 'national character' of the British! How often their 'taste for compromise', their 'sporting spirit in politics', their 'golden mean', their 'pragmatism', their inveterate 'traditionalism' and other stereotypes are invoked! As if these concepts explained everything by dint of repetition, when of course their first characteristic is to explain nothing at all. They also absolve one from asking the real questions, such as why tradition prevailed at one juncture and not at another, why such and such compromise or reform or pressure group won the day and not others. So much repetitive parrot-talk. . . . It behoves us therefore to cast aside all easy and misleading catch-phrases and to press on to *real* analyses by uncovering the *real* forces at work – structures, classes, hierarchies, ethical codes, ideologies, sacred and profane beliefs. There we shall find solid ground for explanations, far from conventional views and superficial clichés. After all, was it not the method followed by our illustrious predecessors, all those French pioneers in the discovery of England who gave us analytical models that were rigorous, profound and penetrating, and whose names were Alexis de Tocqueville, Léon Faucher, Hippolyte Taine, Emile Boutmy, Moïsei Ostrogorski, Paul Mantoux, André Siegfried, André Philip, and of course, greatest of all, Elie Halévy?

Two clarifications to end up with, so as to explain and justify my limits, both in space and time. First of all, I have deliberately chosen to speak of

'English' society. Not that I underestimate the role played by Scotsmen, Welshmen and Irishmen in the development of the kingdom, but until recently, among the British as well as among foreigners the word 'England' certainly had a generic meaning.[7] The best proof is that, up to the nineteenth century, neither the Scots nor the Irish hesitated to use the word to describe the United Kingdom. Even in the twentieth century Bonar Law, though he was half Scottish and half Canadian by birth, had no qualms about calling himself 'Prime Minister of England'. Also, on great historic occasions it is the word 'England' that has always prevailed, from Nelson at Trafalgar ('England expects every man to do his duty') up to Leo Amery shouting the famous plea to Arthur Greenwood, the Opposition spokesman, in the dramatic Commons debate of 2 September 1939 – 'Speak for England!'. The truth is that no term is satisfactory, for even 'Great Britain' is defective, as it excludes Northern Ireland.

In all events I have centred the book on England, but where the destinies of the Scots and the Welsh and even the Irish follow on the destiny of the English, their history has been taken into account. Elsewhere I have left them out, preferring to concentrate on the major partner rather than to let my attention be distracted by particular details. In the same way the Empire has been left out of our field of study, except where its existence affected the national consciousness.

As for the period covered, the choice of 1851 was an obvious one, for the mid-century represented a turning-point for England, when economic conditions were reversed and social stability re-established. From that moment the triumphs of Victorianism could impose itself freely. After the endless storms of the period 1815–50 during which they nearly lost the helm of the storm-tossed ship, the governing classes felt sudden relief that no tidal wave had wrecked the vessel, and they entered calmer waters. Now the 'SS England' could with pride and assurance sail forward with the wind behind her. On the other hand, 1975 seems to mark no visible break in the historical evolution of English society. This being so I would like to look on my description of the years 1955–75 as being tentative, waiting to be completed and indeed revised in the light of future events. For my part I will take refuge behind the authority of Daniel Defoe who, two hundred and fifty years ago, in the preface to his *Tour* made this excellent comment:

> After all that has been said by others, or can be said here, no description of Great Britain can be what we call a finished account, as no clothes can be made to fit a growing child; no picture carry the likeness of a living face; the size of one, and the countenance of the other always altering with time: so no account of a kingdom thus daily altering its countenance can be perfect. . . .'[8]

I The Power and the Glory: 1851–80

1 Industrialism triumphant

The festival of work and industry

1 May 1851. Extraordinary excitement in London. Around Hyde Park the atmosphere is festive. A motley crowd gathers in the spring sunshine – respectable citizens in top hats, working men in cloth caps, tradesmen in their Sunday best, foreigners from all over Europe. Smart turn-outs pass by, and soon high society and all the celebrities are there. Suddenly a party makes its way through the vast assemblage amid loud cheers – it's the Queen! In great state Victoria, accompanied by Prince Albert, arrives at this splendid show which England has put on – the Great Exhibition of London. Silver trumpets sound out under the vault of the Crystal Palace. A solemn prayer invokes 'the ties of peace and friendship among nations', and the sovereign slowly tours the stands of the Exhibition amid the palm-trees and the flowers and the unfurled flags of all nations to the continuous applause of the crowds.

In a letter to her uncle King Leopold of Belgium written the day after this memorable ceremony, Queen Victoria was proudly able to describe 1 May 1851 as 'the greatest day in our history', adding that it was 'the most beautiful and imposing and touching spectacle ever seen'.[1] And Palmerston echoed her feelings: 'a glorious day for England' – words that well conveyed the general feeling of national success. Thanks to the technical progress and creative energy displayed at the Exhibition, the whole country felt itself raised to the forefront of humanity and imbued by Providence with a mission to lead mankind on its way. Was this the pinnacle of the Victorian era? Yes certainly, but even more it was one of the great moments of English history. For to grasp the full significance of the Great Exhibition, the very first of the universal exhibitions (it lasted from May to October 1851 and welcomed 6 million visitors), it is not enough to regard it, for all its brilliance, simply as a display of material progress in England. Certainly it showed off the superiority of England's enterprise, in terms of manufactured goods, trade and capital, as well as the professional ability of her engineers, designers and workpeople. But its importance went much further. For the country which gave birth to the Industrial Revolution, 1851 marked a celebration as well as a turning point.

On the one hand the Great Exhibition celebrated Great Britain's entry into the era of the industrial society. Machinery and town life from now on assumed more importance than the old agrarian civilization. John Bull, the latter-day Prometheus, had won from nature the secret of power, steam taking the place of fire. This time, however, instead of defying the Creator, the might of man remained subservient to Him. The justification of technology, repeated loud and often, was its work for the progress of the species. Thus, hardly had the industrial system made its appearance in the life of the country than it assumed a hallowed role and became closely bound up with morality.

On the other hand the 'Great Exhibition of the Works of Industry of All Nations', to give its correct title, coincided with the start of a phase of great economic prosperity and social peace. What a contrast there was between the 1840s and the 1850s! Ten years of chaos and conflict, dominated by fear and famine (the 'Hungry Forties') were to be followed by ten years of prosperity and confidence, studded with a thousand marvels (the 'Fabulous Fifties'). The prime reason for the Exhibition's success was that it took place in a tranquil atmosphere – peaceful competition between nations abroad and renewed social harmony at home.

From now on the prosperous classes could breathe freely. For the popular outbreaks of yesterday had never ceased to haunt them – Peterloo, 'Captain Swing', the Bristol riots, and just recently the Chartist marches. With these in mind on the eve of the Great Exhibition the pessimists foresaw the worst excesses – pilfering, brawls, even riots. Wouldn't the display of such treasures excite the worst instincts of the mob? Wouldn't criminals from the underworld emerge to take advantage of the occasion? True, the Government took precautions on the opening day. Whole regiments of Hussars and Dragoons, and battalions of Fusiliers were brought in from the provinces to bivouac in the suburbs. Batteries of artillery were kept in reserve in the Tower of London. Several Guards' battalions were massed inside Hyde Park as well as some cavalry. Finally 6,000 policemen were mobilized. However no incident disturbed law and order either that day or at any time during the Exhibition. When the lamps were finally extinguished, the nation was proud to learn that in six months not a flower had been picked!

The attitude of the masses caused surprise at first, but people soon felt reassured and comforted. The social scene had indeed changed. Instead of a Theatre of Cruelty, it was a Theatre of Harmony that held the stage. Had England finally achieved lasting social peace? For twenty years an endless chorus of complaint about pauperism had made itself heard against a backcloth of proletarian squalor, but from 1851 onwards the tune was to change. With one voice everyone sang the praises of hard work and industrial success, and compliments for the workers were the order of the day. Hardly a word was breathed about the 'dangerous classes'; they had now disappeared from the scene. In their place the 'labouring classes' took the limelight. Wasn't it touching to contemplate 'the fustian jackets and unshorn chins of England' enjoying a peaceful picnic on the grass in Hyde Park instead of dreaming of how to overthrow society, when the outward signs of triumphant Capitalism were laid out a few feet away from them?

One must recognize that the Exhibition profited from a combination of favourable circumstances. While general confidence resulted from the strong economic recovery which began in 1851, most of the great battles which used to divide the nation into rival camps had now ceased to rage. With free trade in force since 1846, Chartism in retreat, Irish agitation broken by the failure of the Young Ireland movement, and the tragedy of the Great Famine, classes and parties no longer had the same motives to oppose each other. Somewhat to their surprise but with considerable self-satisfaction Englishmen woke up to the fact that they were almost the only people in Europe to have escaped the disturbing revolutions of 1848. Inevitably the *Zeitgeist* also underwent a profound change. Now was the time for science, the arts, and peace. People were ready to listen attentively to official spokesmen, such as the organizers of the Exhibition, when they affirmed that the future did not lie in Utopian demands or in fratricidal quarrels, but that progress and welfare depended above all on individual effort and on peace, both national and international.

The Exhibition itself was a stupendous festival of technology. The organizers wanted to present a whole panorama of human activity, and to that end divided the exhibits into four sections: raw materials, machinery, manufactured goods and fine arts. But of course the achievements of *homo britannicus*, creator of the first industrial society, were entitled to pride of place. Of the 14,000 exhibitors, 7,400 represented Great Britain and her colonies, and 6,600 the rest of the world. It was a triumph for the Age of the Machine. On every side the primacy of metal and coal asserted itself. People like Ruskin might mourn in vain the transformation of old

England into 'a land of the Iron Mask'.[2] The island had indeed been transformed, as Michelet said, into 'a mass of coal and iron'. The machine reigned supreme. The crowds gaped in admiration at the locomotives, at the models of metal bridges, hydraulic presses, giant lenses for lighthouses, the latest refinements in machine-tools devised by the pioneers in precision engineering (Whitworth, Fairbairn, Armstrong) and the great Nasmyth steam hammer that was able at one moment to come down with the full weight of its 500 tons and at another to crack delicately the shell of an egg. There were machines of every sort – for threshing corn, for crushing sugar cane, for making soda water, for folding envelopes, for rolling cigarettes, and so on.

To technical objectives were added aesthetic and moral ambitions. What the organizers wanted was to unite the useful, the beautiful and the good. On entering the show the visitor was greeted by two symbolic figures: on one side a giant statue of Richard Coeur de Lion, national hero and perfect knight, the personification of courage, and on the other, an enormous block of coal weighting 24 tons, representing power! Some exhibits aimed to unite industry and art, others sought above all to speak to the imagination, from the dazzling 'Crystal Fountain', a transparent structure 10 metres high in the centre of the Exhibition, to the fabulous Crown diamond, the Koh-i-Noor.

Yet, amid all these achievements of the technological age, the most spectacular success was the very building which housed the whole show, the famous Crystal Palace. It was an edifice of staggering dimensions – 520 metres long (three times the length of St Paul's Cathedral), 125 metres wide with a display capacity of 9,000 square metres in which there was plenty of room to arrange the 109,000 exhibits.[3] Withal the building was light and airy, thanks to its construction of metal and glass. A building of genius devised by an amateur self-made man, the former gardener Paxton, the Crystal Palace was a remarkable combination of the classical canons of taste – symmetry and simplicity of design – and the functionalism of modern construction methods. Conceived as a cathedral of industry and designed in the form of a Latin cross with a wide transept, this gigantic temple of glass was at once admired for its imposing beauty. It was greeted with a chorus of praise, accompanied by an abundance of religious parallels. Some saw 'the greatest temple ever built for the arts of peace'. For a German visitor it was the sanctuary of *Weltkultur*. A Frenchman wrote that the old dream of Babel had come to pass, but instead of a mixture of tongues, 'the fusion of interests and minds has been achieved'.[4] An American admirer saw in the Great Exhibition the apocalyptic vision of the New Jerusalem that had appeared to St John on Patmos.[5] Others in more pagan vein talked of a magician's palace.

At the dawn of the new half-century the country was bathed in optimism. There was a firm belief that the year 1851 prefigured an age of peace, progress and universal happiness. The nation was inspired by a grandiose vision of man's power, a power capable of mastering matter without falling into materialism, since his activity was constantly referred to the Almighty. Just as the entrepreneurs and manufacturers at the Exhibition were proud of having achieved a synthesis of beauty and function, so it was asserted that there was no difficulty in reconciling dominion over Nature with surrender to God. Progress and the Bible were not incompatible. The future seemed to belong to those who, like the British, knew how to combine the hand of God with the right arm of Man. In fact all these half-scientific homilies should be interpreted as so much quasi-religious worship of the genius of industry. This was well expressed by the popular poet and song-writer Mackay in the verses set to music by Henry Russell:

> Gather, ye Nations, gather! From forge, and mine, and mill!
> Come, Science and Invention; Come, Industry and Skill!
> Come with your woven wonders, the blossoms of the loom,
> That rival Nature's fairest flowers in all but their perfume.
> Come with your brass and iron, your silver and your gold
> And arts that change the face of earth, unknown to men of old.
> Gather, ye Nations, gather! From ev'ry clime and soil,
> The New Confederation, the Jubilee of toil.[6]

There is another lesson to be drawn from the Great Exhibition if you take it as the symbol of an emergent industrial system. The triumph of the machine launched the era of the masses. Some acute minds understood it at the time, and the Great Exhibition gave a foretaste of that era on the material as well as the human level. Everything was multiplied both in manufacture and in selling. Development progressed rapidly, from the making of one object, or possibly a hundred, to a thousand and then a million. Who had ever imagined standardization on such a scale as to produce 300,000 plates of glass to build the Crystal Palace, all of identical shape and size, or the sale on the refreshment stand of a million bottles of soda-water, lemonade and ginger beer, all manufactured by the house of Schweppes? In the *Revue des Deux Mondes*, a French visitor to the Exhibition commented subtly on England's success in adapting herself to the necessities of mass consumption, while France continued to specialize in producing for the luxury market: 'It is very odd. An aristocratic country like England is successful at supplying the people, whereas France, a democratic country, is only good at producing goods for the aristocracy!'[7]

On the human level too, quantity was the dominant theme. The railways and technical improvements meant that crowds of people could come together in a way that had never before been seen. In this respect the Great Exhibition was a huge popular festival – a real party for the people. It was the opposite of the splendid displays at Versailles or Windsor which were reserved for a small privileged circle. This was a democratic show laid on for the inquisitive masses gathered together in festive mood. It was not simply a deliberate (and successful) attempt on the part of Prince Albert, the chief organizer of the enterprise, to build a bridge between the monarchy and the machine, between the court and the labouring masses. For at the same time it managed to unite all classes, especially the workers, in their admiration for the industrial system, and this integrated the whole nation into the structure of a 'liberal' society. That was the political significance of the Exhibition. It conferred a smiling appearance on a dominating Capitalism and adorned it with every crea-tive virtue. The trading economy, now launched on its triumphant career, could ignore the odd signs of revolt that cropped up here and there, and could concentrate on drawing the maximum profit from the successes of industrialism.

So it was from sound knowledge that one of the most influential celebrators of progress and the liberal destiny of England, the great Whig historian Macaulay, asserted that 1851 'will long be remembered as a singularly happy year of peace, plenty, good feeling, innocent pleasure, national glory of the best and purest sort'.[8] Who then showed concern for the other side of the coin? Who paid attention to the victims – the multitude of the crushed and the oppressed? Who noticed that in that same year, in the heart of Africa, the soldiers of Her Majesty were engaged in bloody battles to annex the country of the Kaffirs to the Empire and turn poor black peasants off their lands? Who felt indignant that on Christmas Day 1851 it was necessary to organize a charity gather-ing in the heart of London, at Leicester Square, so that 10,000 poor families of the district could have a bit of roast beef and plum pudding washed down with a cup of tea?

Unlimited growth

'With Steam and the Bible the English traverse the globe' was the proud boast of one of the Great Exhibition guides.[9] Indeed the growth of the economy seemed miraculous. The national income was multiplied by eight in the course of the century, while the population only went up by four. A doubling of the income per head occurred in the second half of the century. The great 'Victorian prosperity' began in 1851 under the influ-ence of the world rise in prices, and it went on until 1873. Even the difficult times after that date did not halt this dynamic progress. In the thirty years between 1851 and 1881 the national product rose from £523 million (£25 per inhabitant) to £1,051 million (£35 per inhabitant).[10]

Each key sector showed an advance. Exports? They were £55 million in 1840–9; they went up to £100 million in 1850–9, to £160 million in 1860–9 and to £218 million in 1870–9. Railways? 6,000 miles had already been built by 1850; in 1870 the total had reached 14,000 miles. Cotton? Imports of raw cotton (the best gauge of textile activity) increased in weight from 300 million lbs in 1830–9 to 800 million in 1850–9, to 1,250 million in 1870–9. The merchant fleet? The tonnage of British shipping plying the world was 3.6 million in 1850; it was 6.6 million in 1880, of which 40 per cent was steam against less than 5 per cent in 1850. Metals? The production of cast iron rose from 2 million tons in 1850 to 6 million in 1875.[11] In all directions it was a breathless, almost intoxicating race for growth and profit. Coalmines, foundries, blast furnaces, shipyards, cotton mills, woollen mills, linen and jute factories, arsenals, cement works, cutlery workshops, makers of shoes, precision instruments and furniture, all competed with each other to produce goods more and more cheaply and exported them to the four corners of the earth. Hence the proud feeling of success, smugly expressed by the inventor of the term 'Victorian'. 'The Englishman lives . . . to move and to struggle, to conquer and to build; to visit all seas, to diffuse the genius of his character over all nations. Industry, Protestantism, Liberty, seem born of the Teutonic race – that race to whom God has committed the conservation as well as the spread of Truth and on whom mainly depend the civilization and progress of the world.'[12]

These were the external signs of growth. We must now analyse its effects so that we can try to extract an answer to the question – why was England supreme? For the key result of that growth from a macro-economic point of view, was England's dominant position in the world, a position which was only reinforced by the advances of the period 1850–75. In the middle of the century the country entered what Walter Rostow has described as the 'mature' stage, that is to say that it was now able to produce beyond the key 'take-off' sectors by applying techniques of management and accumulated investments to a wide variety of economic activities. As a nation on the move Great Britain was continuously able to extend her resources and strengthen her leading position. That is why she was variously called 'the Workshop of the World', 'the Industry State' and even 'the Fuel State'.

Thanks to the alliance of industry and commerce, to entrepreneurial skill and tenacity, to individual enterprise and the collective guarantees of *Pax Britannica*, England drew advantage from a whole range of economic stimuli. Sure of herself and of the blessing of heaven, she not only outstripped all other nations including the most highly industrialized, but it was often she who stimulated their development. In 1860 England produced nearly 60 per cent of the coal and steel in the world, more than

50 per cent of the cast iron and nearly 50 per cent of the cotton goods. In 1870 the United Kingdom produced one third of the world output of manufactured goods, and the national income per inhabitant was higher than in any other country. The French, although relatively rich, achieved only 60 per cent of the average individual income of the English. To illustrate this supremacy one can simply quote individual cases; for instance the railway construction magnate Thomas Brassey who, in twenty-five years, built 7,000 kilometres of line over four continents. The great bankers of the City competed in power with crowned heads, whom Disraeli described admiringly as 'mighty moneylenders whose *fiat* some-times held in balance the destinies of kings and empires'.[13] Among the key-points of European development it was the London-Birmingham-Manchester axis that held the lead without serious rival. In his book *L'Europe sans rivages*, F. Perroux powerfully evoked the extraordinary thrust of British trade which, with the support of the City of London, permeated the arteries and circulation of world commerce, continuously extended it bounds of influence, centralized information and banking facilities, and fixed prices that were expressed in a dominant currency, i.e. sterling, which was everyone's favourite. Such was the supreme power and leadership of a nation which 'living rather grandly, having worked hard and possessing immense strength, . . . could address the world'.[14]

We must now try to understand the overall reasons for this growth and progress: what are the factors that explain English supremacy at this time? One must hark back to the past to answer this question. For it is beyond doubt that the English in the middle of the nineteenth century continued to draw full benefit from the series of advantages which had made their country the cradle of the Industrial Revolution. Only they were not simply content to hang on to those trumps they held in their hands at the outset. The combination of a multiplying and accelerating upward growth gave the British economy an even faster impetus and rhythm than any other, and placed her in a leading position ahead of all competitors.

The list of advantages enjoyed by prosperous Albion is a long one: a remarkable abundance of natural resources thanks to a sub-soil rich in coal and iron-ore, many waterways, a climate favourable to textile fibres, surrounding seas at the cross-roads of the world's trade-routes; a strong current of innovation that encouraged advanced techniques with high productivity, supported by well-qualified engineers, technicians and workmen; a trade network of proven value with vast foreign markets spread over five continents, and a colonial empire both rich and exten-sive, all served by a merchant fleet without rival in number and variety of vessels; a vast accumulation of capital and profitable investments; ample

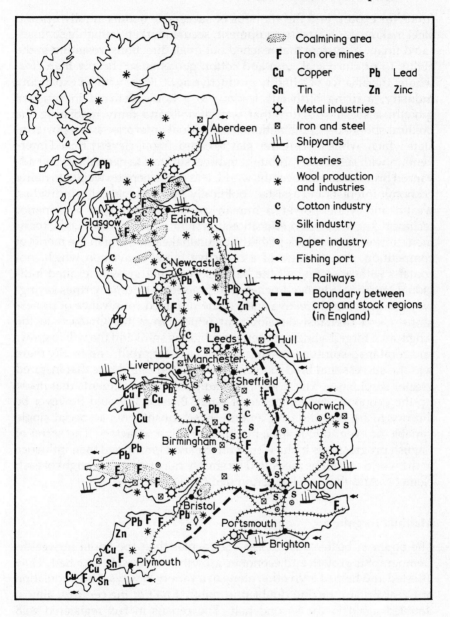

Map 1.   Economic geography of Great Britain in 1851

The demarcation line (taken from Caird) separates the pastures from the arable lands in England – the stock-raising areas (with high rents) in the west, and the lands under cultivation in the east.

funds for export, and the stimulus of successive booms in railways and steel making; high quality equipment, secure markets, a highly sophisticated financial system that reached out in all directions, resulting in the ability to produce coal, iron and cotton goods more cheaply than elsewhere; the alliance of a highly productive agriculture with an expanding industry; a rising birth-rate leading to a home demand in constant growth; a social structure that was flexible and fairly mobile; in the political sphere the combination of individual enterprise and a powerful state which, while leaving free play to competition, cleverly mixed intervention with *laissez-faire*, brought indirect support to everything that advanced British interests over the world, lent parliamentary weight to ruling economic interests and assisted, politically and diplomatically, individual wealth and world power; a human capital characterized by superior technical know-how; an educational system which encouraged experiment, innovation and adaptability; an unshakeable belief in the merits of competition; the pressure of a collective moral conviction which, not content with upsetting all the barriers opposing growth, exalted individual initiative, idealized riches, and praised as cardinal virtues saving, work, mobility and creative energy; the unforced connivance of protestantism and capitalist development which, from the Quakers to the Anglicans, forged a link between the religious spirit and the will to grow, and combined spiritual strivings with a taste for profit; and finally there was the success that bred more success and the confidence that inspired greater confidence. These were the multifarious constituents that made up the economic pre-eminence of Great Britain. It would however be illusory to try and discover among these constituents a special single variable or even to look for a hierarchy of diverse factors. The secret of English progress was in the web of interrelated forces, and their influence in the world cannot be measured by simply calculating the weight of each element. And that is what astounded the world.

Malthus forgotten

The boom in births was no less spectacular than the boom in wealth. Demographic growth and economic growth were closely matched. They affected and helped each other along in a variety of ways. The population of Great Britain, having doubled in the first half of the century, almost doubled again in the second half. The census in fact registered 20.8 million inhabitants in 1851 (as opposed to 10.5 million in 1801) and 37 million in 1901. If one looks at the three 'nations' of the island, one sees that England has the lion's share with 16.9 million souls in 1851 (against 8.3 million in 1801) and 30.8 million in 1901. The Welsh, who numbered half a million at the end of the eighteenth century, reached 1 million in

1851 and 1.7 million in 1901. Here the population explosion was accompanied by a remarkable geographical concentration, for by 1901 half the population were living in the county of Glamorgan. The latter had more inhabitants than the other eleven Welsh counties put together, whereas in 1851 it contained only 10 per cent of the total. In Scotland, where emigration had a greater effect and where the population also tended to concentrate in one region, the Lowlands, the number of inhabitants increased at a slower rate. There were 2.9 million Scotsmen in 1851 (as opposed to 1.6 million in 1801) and 4.5 million in 1901 – an increase of 55 per cent compared with increases of 69 per cent in Wales and 82 per cent in England.

The rhythm of its increase kept Great Britain at the head of the European league. She maintained the ample lead she had won at the time of the population explosion. From 1851 to 1881 her annual rate of increase, which was around 1.3 per cent, put her at the head of Europe, equal to Holland and Denmark, well above Prussia, Belgium, Italy and Russia, and leaving France a long way behind. Having underlined demographic potency as a major trait of British society, one ought perhaps to spell out its elements. It was the coexistence of three characteristics which gave the population of England in the middle of the nineteenth century its particularly original make-up: a number of old persistent patterns dating from the pre-industrial demographic regime, a stabilization of the forces at work in the great flood of growth, and finally new migration movements heading overseas.

Table 1 The age distribution of the population of England and Wales, 1821–1971

	1821	1851	1881	1911	1931	1951	1971
0–9 years	27.9	24.8	25.7	20.9	15.8	15.7	16.8
10–19 years	21.1	20.5	20.6	19.0	16.6	12.6	14.2
20–29 years	15.7	17.5	16.8	17.3	17.1	14.2	14.1
30–39 years	11.8	13.2	12.7	15.3	14.7	14.6	11.6
40–49 years	9.4	9.8	9.8	11.5	13.1	14.9	12.5
50–59 years	6.6	6.9	7.0	8.0	11.1	12.1	12.0
over 60 years	7.5	7.3	7.4	8.0	11.6	15.9	18.8
	100.0	100.0	100.0	100.0	100.0	100.0	100.0

Among the long-standing characteristics one must mention the preponderance of young age groups, the traditional structure of households and the general fertility. A young country (in 1871 four out of five Englishmen were under 45 and one out of two were under 21), England maintained an age pyramid until after 1880 which was very similar to the one that prevailed, according to Gregory King's estimates, at the end of the seventeenth century. There was the same proportion of young people and probably much the same proportion of elderly. There was little practice of birth control. As for the average size of households, far from showing a new style of family (i.e. smaller families instead of extended families), the works of Peter Laslett have shown a steady continuity from the seventeenth to the end of the nineteenth century – 4.7 persons per household in 1851, the same as the average between 1650 and 1750.[15] Contrary to what has often been thought, not only did industrialism and urbanization contribute nothing to a reduction in the size of households (in fact just the opposite, as the urban family in the nineteenth century tended to be a bit larger than the classic rural family) but indeed recent evidence shows that the composition of households simply followed the traditional model. Only a minority of households extended over three generations and included collateral relations (i.e. aunts, nephews cousins); most of the time they were 'nuclear' families, centred on two generations. Michael Anderson's detailed study of Preston, a typical industrial town in Lancashire, whose family size was noticeably larger than the national average (5.4 persons per household) still showed that three-quarters of the families consisted only of parents and children.[16]

In this great population explosion, which has been called the 'demographic revolution', everyone knows that the central mechanism was the variable effect of three factors: birth-rate, death-rate and marriage-rate. In mid-nineteenth-century England, one sees these factors becoming relatively stable. Between 1840 and 1880 the curves on the graph hardly vary at all. Hence the numerical expansion was both strong and regular.

After the slow decline in the first third of the century the death-rate seems to have reached a plateau at around 22–3 per 'ooo. No doubt the plateau tilts downwards a little, but until 1875 there is no decisive alteration to be seen. Neither public health nor medical science brought about a spectacular change. Infant mortality did not vary. Another proof of stability was the insignificant change in life expectancy. While in 1841 it was 40 years for men and 42 years for women, it increased by only one or two points in the course of the next thirty years and only just reached 44 years and 48 years at the end of the century. On the marriage side, i.e. marriage-rate and average age of marriage, the fluctuations were insignificant. Finally the birth-rate kept up its high level with splendid regularity, for the five-year averages remained consistently between 35 and 36 per 'ooo up to 1875.

The result of all this was that the demographic factors, which more or less stabilized just before the mid-century, remained unaltered until 1880 and resulted in a remarkable increase in numbers. Around that date

300,000 new souls were added to the population of Great Britain every year. The main reason for this was the large gap between the number of births and the number of deaths – three births for every two deaths. For one birth followed another pell-mell. In the public mind the traditional picture of the family reigned supreme. The large family was the rule. Wasn't it the law of nature? For example in the cohort of marriages celebrated between 1861 and 1869, amounting to a million and a half couples, an average of 6.2 children was produced.[17] At this time more than one family out of six consisted of 10 children or more. On the other hand only one out of eight families had 1 or 2 children.

Fertility, vitality, activity – the social side of life echoed the biological. This outpouring of young human beings required new horizons and a field of expansion broader than an island with a rising population could offer. The national territory was not enough. Energy and ambition sought fresh territories overseas in which to work. There was, of course a long tradition of distant trade and pioneer colonization, but there was a change of scale in the middle of the nineteenth century. Emigration, occurring in successive waves (1851–4, 1863–6, 1869–74, 1880–4) became a prodigious phenomenon.

Up until 1840 the flow of departures had stayed at a modest level; and emigrants had been recruited mostly from the Celtic lands. From then onwards there was a distinct change. Emigration absorbed at least one third of the excess of births over deaths. And it was now England's turn, after Scotland and Ireland, to become an important source of leavers. It is certainly difficult to arrive at an accurate number of people who left their native land for good, because many returned and the statistics do not distinguish between the different subjects of the United Kingdom. Nevertheless we can reckon that the number of English and Scots who left between 1850 and 1880 to people the new Anglo-Saxon lands came to more than 3 million. If the currents of emigration (in which a distinct preponderance of males must be noted – three out of five) had their ups and downs of intensity, they showed a striking regularity in their destinations. Two-thirds of emigrants started life again in the United States, one-fifth in Australia and New Zealand, one-tenth in Canada. Around 1875–80 we see a new current, albeit a very small one, towards South Africa. The preference for America persisted steadily until 1895. The change only came about in the last years of the century, when quite quickly the share of the United States dropped to half of the total and then declined further, to the advantage of Canada and South Africa. So all over the world there sprang up Anglo-Saxon homes where myriad links were kept up with the motherland in the spheres of finance and exchange, of sentiment and institutions, of religion and culture, and of language and civilization.

At the same time emigration appeared as a remedy for pauperism and economic difficulties. It offered a safety-valve to the threat of social breakdown. It provided an outlet which channelled both the despair of the unemployed and the appetite of those who looked for profitable ventures; and in addition it accorded a special means of spreading English influence throughout the world and of making the human capital of the nation bear fruit – 'the best affair of business in which the capital of an old and wealthy country can engage' said John Stuart Mill.[18] In his *Notes on England*, Taine recounts with admiration a meeting with two young people, born into a family of twelve children, who are getting ready to leave for New Zealand to be sheep farmers: 'Impossible to describe their energy, their ardour, their decisiveness . . . one feels a superabundance of energy and activity, an overflowing of animal spirits.' He concludes: 'Here is a fine way of entering life. Many risks are taken, the world is wide open, and one skims off the cream.'[19]

For side by side with the hunger that drove the surplus mouths overseas there existed a well-to-do emigration, less numerous but very active. This was the emigration of managers who went out to Egypt, to India, to the Rio de la Plata or to China. In the four corners of the globe you came across these pioneers, on the Colorado as well as on the Yangtse, in Lagos or Beirut, in Winnipeg or Singapore. For some of them expatriation was only temporary. They intended to come back home after a few years, their fortunes made, or at least having accumulated a modest pile. For others it was a departure for good, sometimes cheerful, sometimes endured with resignation and that sadness which one sees in the faces of Ford Madox Brown's painting, 'The Last of England'.

Creative energy was thus abounding everywhere, abroad as well as at home. Growth gave rise to enterprise, which in its turn bred confidence for further ventures. Travel, which for some meant a voyage as far as the Antipodes, became the symbol of a society of movement, adventure and expansion.

On the urban front

As the first country to arrive at an industrial civilization, England was also the first to experience a predominantly urban way of life – the one that was to become the lot of all the advanced nations. Her peculiar experience was to arrive at this stage very early and at the same time on a massive scale. Indeed it was around 1845 that the traditional town-country pattern was reversed. The long domination of the country then came to an end, and the predominance of towns started. Once this tendency had got under way, the imbalance in favour of towns very rapidly asserted itself. The urban population, which just formed the majority in 1851, was very far ahead 40 years later, when three English-men out of four were townsmen. In less than half a century England became an urban nation. But in this leap forward the change was not simply numerical. The transformation was even more one of the quality of life than of mere numbers. In the course of this urbanization a new visual scene emerged together with a new system of social relations and a new lifestyle – in brief a new civilization came into being.

Table 2 Urban and rural populations in England and Wales in the nineteenth century[20]

	Urban and rural populations as a percentage of the total population								
	1801	1841	1851	1861	1871	1881	1891	1901	1911
THE POPULATION LIVING IN TOWNS									
of over 100,000 inhabitants	11.0	20.7	24.8	28.8	32.6	36.2	39.4	43.6	43.8
of 50,000 – 100,000 inhabitants	3.5	5.5	5.9	6.1	5.6	7.3	8.6	7.5	8.0
of 20,000 – 50,000 inhabitants	4.8	6.8	7.0	7.4	9.6	9.4	9.2	9.9	10.4
of 10,000 – 20,000 inhabitants	4.7	5.3	6.4	6.6	6.6	6.6	7.1	8.1	7.9
of 2,500 – 10,000 inhabitants	9.8	10.0	9.9	9.8	10.8	10.5	10.2	8.9	8.8
TOTAL URBAN POPULATION	33.8	48.3	54.0	58.7	65.2	70.0	74.5	78.0	78.9
TOTAL RURAL POPULATION	76.2	51.7	46.0	41.3	34.8	30.0	25.5	22.0	21.1
No. of towns with over 100,000 inhabitants	1	7	10£	13	17	20	24	33	36
No. of towns with 20,000 – 100,000 inhabitants	16	48	55	66	88	108	118	141	165

The urban front now developed three special characteristics – fast rhythm of growth, new types of living quarters and a new ordering of space. To take growth first, the rate was so remarkable that one can only talk of galloping urbanization, and the figures bear this out eloquently. Table 2 shows on the one hand the spectacular rise of the urban population (in absolute terms it tripled between 1850 and 1900), and on the other hand the supremacy of the large towns in the expansion.

Side by side with the large towns whose wealth dated from the beginning of the Industrial Revolution (between 1851 and 1901 Manchester grew from 340,000 inhabitants to 650,000, and its huge suburb, Salford, from 65,000 to 220,000; the Liverpool area went up from 400,000 to 700,000, the Birmingham area from 230,000 to 760,000; in Scotland, Glasgow leapt from 360,000 to 920,000) one can see the swift rise of towns of second rank, which assumed the role of regional capitals. In the second half of the century Leeds increased from 170,000 to 430,000, Sheffield from 135,000 to more than 400,000, Newcastle from 90,000 to 250,000 and Hull from 85,000 to 240,000. Others held their old positions, e.g. Bristol with 330,000 inhabitants in 1901 as against 140,000 half a century earlier. Among the fastest growing towns we should mention Leicester, in the

Midlands, (60,000 souls in 1850, 210,000 in 1901) where new engineering industries joined the traditional hosiery activity; Stoke-on-Trent in the heart of the Potteries, up from 65,000 to 215,000; and the textile centres of Nottingham and Derby. Some towns rose up out of nothing. Coal created Cardiff, ironworks Middlesborough and Barrow-in-Furness, the railways Crewe and Swindon.

Throughout the country, apart from the extreme north of England and Scotland, there was one prevalent type of habitation: that of the individual house. The 1851 census remarks on this subject that 'the possession of an entire house is strongly desired by every Englishman, for it throws a sharp, well-defined circle round his family and hearth – the shrine of his sorrows, joy, and meditations.'[21] This indicates a profound longing for domestic independence, expressed even by humble folk in the well-known saying 'my home is my castle'. Of course living quarters of this kind tended to give rise to an individualist mentality, without lessening in working-class areas a lively spirit of solidarity and mutual help among families.

Houses varied considerably in size and comfort according to the social class and income of the occupants. In middle-class areas one found terrace houses next to each other all along a street, or detached houses standing in their own large gardens. The latter style was favoured by the more prosperous families, being a vision of the aristocratic country house on a small scale. A more economic solution was often adopted in the lower levels of the middle class – pairs of 'semi-detached' houses joined together and separated from their neighbours. The spacious Victorian terrace houses, usually built in the classical style with a profusion of columns, balconies and stucco facings but occasionally displaying the Hanseatic, Flemish or Tudor mode, were nearly always built with an identical interior plan. The distribution of rooms was an exact reflection of the orders of society. The lower classes, i.e. the servants, for their day-time work occupied the basement ('below stairs') where the kitchen, the pantry and the servants' hall were situated, and in the evening they went up to the third or fourth floors to sleep. The ground floor and the first two floors were the domain of the masters. The dining-room and an occasional room were usually on the ground-floor; the drawing-room, where the lady of the house presided, was on the first floor; and the bedrooms of the parents and children on the second floor.

In the poorer quarters, i.e. in most of the town, the workers' dwellings also followed a more or less fixed plan. They nearly always consisted of small two-floor brick houses, aligned in terraces and separated from the next row at the back by a small yard or a bit of garden. These houses sometimes had two rooms on each floor, but more often a single room or 'one up, one down'. From the end of the eighteenth century onwards, it also often happened that the builders took to backing houses one against the other to save ground. This 'back-to-back' technique was a calamity denounced by all experts in hygiene, which is why from 1850 onwards most local authorities ruled out the system, but the back-to-backs took a long time to disappear. In Nottingham for example, around 1850, there were 8,000 such houses, i.e. two-thirds of the dwellings in the town. The scourge of urban squalor was not confined to this type of construction. Slums resulted from overcrowding, itself the product of poverty and high rents, and from 'jerry-building', a cut-price way of building on badly drained soil with no solid foundations and using materials of poor quality. The result was that whole districts were made up of hovels without air or water, and without sanitation beyond a common sewer. Rubbish and filth gathered in these fetid cess-pits, and encouraged vermin and epidemics of every kind. Urban misery reached the depths of degradation.

Property speculation played an important role in the development of towns. First it was a fruitful sector for investment because of rapid expansion. The return on building was a regular 6 per cent. At the same time the fast growth of the towns gave a boost to ground values which continued to be high and on the increase even up to our own times. However, quite apart from the effect of rising land values, the spatial layout and the Victorian urban scene are above all explained by the system of land ownership and the methods of building development. The ground landlords often possessed vast estates. When a landlord decided to parcel out all or part of his property, he usually got in touch with a 'speculative builder' who took charge of the development.

There were two consequences to this. First of all, the uniform appearance of urban houses in England – mass-produced, all the houses in the same street or the same district resemble one another in design and size. The resulting impression is one of monotony which strikes all foreigners. Bernstein recalls in his memoirs that Marx, who was very short-sighted, regularly entered the wrong house when he came back to his district of Kentish Town from the British Museum.[22] Secondly the landlord, whether he was a private individual or an institution, usually imposed a general scheme for the construction of the houses and the street lay-out, together with a mass of specifications, so that, paradoxically, private initiative tempered the natural anarchy of urban development. It is therefore, a mistake to suppose that Victorian towns were simply the products of chance. At the estate level they were not without plan or direction. *Laissez-faire* and the profit motive were joined together to produce a certain degree of control. It would be more sensible to talk of a mosaic of small enterprises rubbing shoulders with one another, a curious mixture of order in detail and chaos in the general plan. Victorian town development was thus tempered by a degree of private planning which took over some of the traditions of the aristocratic urbanism of the classic period. In the end, towards the close of the century, public authority planning started to assert itself.

This form of 'mosaic' development inevitably led to each district, and even each street in a town, acquiring a special character, and so gave rise to social segregation. Even before it was built one could see the destiny fixed for an area, and in a social system as strictly defined and hierarchical as Victorian England, the differentiation became mandatory. It is well known that every town reflects in its layout and architecture the society from which it springs. In Great Britain's case the methods of town development as well as the prevalence of horizontal construction led to an urban geography that underlined social divisions more than in any other country. Far from bringing different social groups together, the British town contributed to isolation, not to say apartheid. There was indeed a contradiction here with the ambitions of society which aimed, as we shall see, at a closing of the ranks round a political and moral consensus. On the contrary, urban life led to local loyalty – to the neighbourhood, to the street, to the group of houses or the district – and to the strengthening of class distinctions. As against this the extreme diversity of the towns – large conurbations like Manchester, Birmingham or Glasgow, medium-sized industrial cities like Halifax, Huddersfield or Barrow-in-Furness, small peaceful towns like York or Oxford, resorts like Brighton or Scarborough, etc. – led to a host of regional and local nuances.

London

Standing apart, in a class by itself, was the capital – the 'Metropolis'. It was an enormous mass which by its extent and the number of its inhabitants and buildings far outstripped all other towns in the world, without a possible rival. London seemed to be the incarnation of the Industrial Age. Its population passed the million mark when the century was just two years old. It was the first town since the fall of Rome to reach this total. In 1851 there were 2.4 million Londoners; in 1881 there were 3.8 million, and for the whole conurbation of Greater London the total was even 4,750,000. It was at the turn of the century that the town itself, i.e. the County of London, reached its maximum of 4.5 million according to the census of 1901, while Greater London, whose growth was no less spectacular, counted 6.6 million inhabitants. This ocean of houses stretching as far as the eye could reach induced a feeling of immensity that almost overwhelmed the beholder – a source of fear as well as of admiration. The vision that constantly sprang to the minds of the Victorians was that of the great cities of antiquity, such as Tyre, Nineveh, Palmyra, and, above all, Babylon. Byron's phrase 'the modern Babylon' became the standard way to express, depending on the context, the grandeur, the power, the wealth, the vice or the corruption of this monster city. When Ozanam visited London for the 1851 Exhibition, he saw there, after Rome and Paris, 'the third capital of modern civilization'. Most Englishmen, being less eclectic and more jingoist, soon set up their own clichés and described their capital as 'the centre-point of the civilized world', 'the wonderful centre of the world's trade', or, alluding to the gigantic concentration of wealth 'the Golden City'. London was represented as the microcosm of the universe, 'the World City'.

However, the concentration was so vast and so diverse, so fragmented and contrasted, that it was difficult to form a concrete idea of the whole. Mayhew, the most famous researcher of the mid-century, had the notion of trying an ascent in a balloon above the giant town. From that special vantage-point he observed in fascination the 'Leviathan metropolis with a dense canopy of smoke hanging over it'. But even from there it was impossible, he reported, 'to tell where the monster city began or ended, for the buildings stretched not only to the horizon on either side, but far away into the distance . . . where the town seemed to blend into the sky'. He went into ecstacies at the sight of 'this vast bricken mass of churches and hospitals, banks and prisons, palaces and workhouses, docks and refuges for the destitute, parks and squares, and courts and alleys, which make up London'. Indeed the observer was struck less by the quantities of houses than by the countless mass of human beings of all conditions, assembled in this small area where the threads of millions of human destinies crossed each other. At this level social analysis, as so often happened in that moralizing age, was coloured by ethical considerations of the good and bad results of such a concentration of humanity, a 'strange conglomeration of vice, avarice and low cunning, of noble aspirations and humble heroism'. From his balloon the journalist, comparing his airy position to that of an 'angel's view' takes to meditating on this 'huge town where perhaps there is more virtue and more iniquity, more wealth and more want, brought together in one dense focus than in any other part of the earth'.[23]

The area of the town continued to spread like an oil patch advancing by capillarity, with some fingers shooting out along the axes of the main roads and railways. In its gradual advance the town engulfed ancient villages, market gardens and pastures, driving farms and their fields ever further out. Urbanization took over whole tracts of land in its progress. Private estates, often of considerable acreage, were suddenly given over to development. In this way the fashionable new districts of Kensington and Paddington, extending the West End further west, were constructed, while to the north substantial houses sprang up in St John's Wood, Hampstead and Islington. On the east side and on the flat lands south of the Thames, the working-class quarters predominated with their long monotonous lines of small grey houses. The East End grew towards Mile End, Poplar and Hackney, while on the south bank of the river the spaces between the ancient boroughs of Southwark and Greenwich were filled

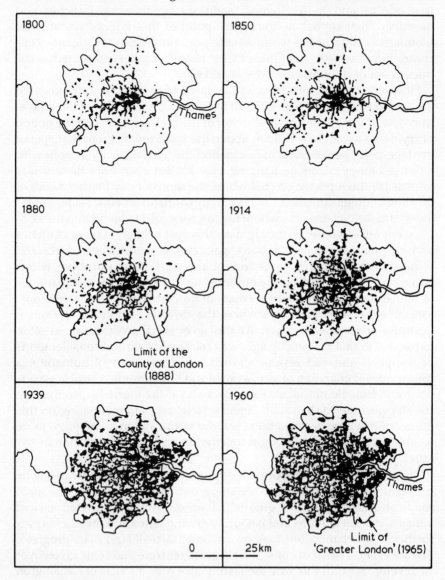

Map 2.   The growth of London[24]

in with housing, and new districts such as Battersea and Camberwell developed at the same pace. Further south, near the first line of Surrey hills, the solid suburbs rose up amid greenery, with their comfortable detached villas in the middle of large shady gardens.

What was completely new from the mid-century onwards was the movement of the population away from the central districts. The zone most affected was the City and its adjacent areas. While the City's population from 1801 to 1851 was very stable with an almost constant figure of 130,000 inhabitants (which gave a considerable density – over 1,000 people per acre on average, and in certain areas up to nearly 2,000), it suffered a rapid decline in the second half of the century as a result of the building of railway stations and even more of the growth of warehouses and office blocks. In 1881 there were no more than 51,000 inhabitants, in 1901 27,000. The City started to live on a double rhythm – a diminishing night population and a day population of growing numbers and frenzied activity. A 'day census' revealed the daytime presence of 170,000 people in 1866 and 300,000 in 1891.[25] A similar pattern developed in other parts of the historic heart of London – the Strand, Holborn, Soho. In all, between 1851 and 1881, the central districts lost 135,000 people, and towards the end of the century the process was even more rapid. So began a special division of urban space which in the twentieth century was to lead to a contrast between business centres and residential areas, as well as to daily migrations that became both more numerous and longer in distance. However, in the second half of the nineteenth century, these daily journeys were on a small scale – they amounted to less than 50,000 in 1854.[26] Only the well-to-do, i.e. those who had the means to use the omnibus, the train or better still the personal vehicle, could allow themselves to live at a certain distance from their work. All the rest, and particularly the workmen who travelled on foot, were forced to find lodgings near their place of work, with all that this entailed for popular housing – overcrowding, high rents and the spread of slums.

Two phenomena dominated the organization of collective living in London: the total absence of municipal government at town level, and the violence of urban contrasts. London was a huge sprawl without unity, broken up into a multitude of small autonomous districts – civil parishes governed by vestries, unrepresentative and without effective powers. The capital suffered from its division between the City on the one hand, administered by its 'Corporation', a closed oligarchy of businessmen with age-old prestige, and on the other the chaos, not to say anarchy, of a mass of small local authorities, entangled, inefficient and often corrupt – the 'Bumbledom' denounced by Dickens. Until 1888 no remedy was applied to the scandalous under-administration and under-equipment of the world's largest town, for the only reform ever voted (The Metropolis

Management Act of 1855 creating the Metropolitan Board of Works) confined itself to correcting the worst abuses relating to drainage and traffic.

Laissez-faire likewise triumphed in the social sphere. Hence the astonishing contrasts which surprised every visitor. Firstly there were the contrasts between districts. The town was in effect made up of various towns. So it took in the City, world centre of finance and trade, Westminster, the headquarters of the government and heart of the Empire, the industrial zones of the centre and the East End (where garments, shoes, jewels, furniture, silk and timber were made up, and where boats, vehicles, precision instruments, etc. were manufactured) and the south whose specialities were machine-tools, tanning, fire-arms and so on. Beyond London Bridge started the Docks, an immense and very active port, the first in the world. To these wharves and warehouses ships would steam, carrying cargoes from the four corners of the globe: tea, ivory, spices, wine, wood, furs, grain and coal. There was a ceaseless movement of ships on the Thames, an everchanging scene which the brush of Whistler immortalized around 1860 in a series of watercolours. 'A wonderful medley of masts, sails and rigging', remarked Baudelaire, 'a chaos of fog, furnaces and gushing smoke – the profound and complicated poetry of a vast capital.'[27]

Another contrast, and a much more violent one, was the marked difference between opulence and poverty, which went far beyond the standard antithesis of West End and East End. The lines of social hierarchy were drawn with great precision. In 1851, only one Londoner in twenty-five belonged to the 'upper-class', while the 'lower classes', of which the vast majority were manual workers, formed more than four-fifths of the population. In the fine houses of the aristocracy of Belgravia and Mayfair there were parties and a social life of exceptional brilliance, especially in 'the Season', while every day, in Hyde Park, Rotten Row provided an elegant meeting-place for the gentlemen and ladies of society when mounted on horseback. Yet, not a mile from these glamorous scenes where money flowed like water, there were thousands of human beings squatting in filth and misery. Apart from the pockets of poverty which were dotted about the wealthy districts, there were whole areas delivered over to the poor, nearly all the East End and the area that bordered the Thames on the south. Yet, to counter current romantic visions of 'the mysteries of London', we must carefully distinguish between two categories of population. On the one hand there was the majority made up of workmen and small tradespeople who, in spite of conditions that were difficult and often sombre, did manage to make some sort of a living and had no contact with the world of crime. On the other, there was the underworld, whose size and influence has often been unduly exaggerated. It is certainly true that the size and anonymity of the English capital encouraged the existence of a host of castaways and down-and-outs. There were crowds of bad hats, young criminals escaped from detention, sailors who had jumped their ships, pickpockets, prostitutes from innumerable brothels, and above all the left-overs of a society that was merciless to the unfortunate. There were cripples, hard-core unemployed, beggars in rags, hangers around soup-kitchens and night shelters – in short, a world of outsiders on the margin of society, a latent menace to law and order. It was a universe of the starving and destitute which charitable organizations, always anxious to preserve respectability, tended to keep in existence rather than alleviate. It took an optimistic liberal economist like MacCulloch to calculate that one Londoner out of six died in a workhouse, a hospital or a lunatic asylum.

So one can see why the maelstrom of London provoked views that were so passionate and so contradictory. These opinions varied from the invective of critics like Ruskin who spoke of 'that great foul city – rattling, growling, smoking, stinking – a ghastly heap of fermenting brickwork, pouring out poison at every pore',[28] to the enthusiasm of the admirers of a varied and fascinating town, a true epitome of England at the peak of liberalism. It was to the latter that Henry James belonged when he saw in the movement of the capital 'the rumble of the tremendous human mill'.

Green England: the unchanging countryside

The spectacular advance of the towns should not lead us into thinking that the countryside was fading away. In hundreds of ways, directly or indirectly, the old green England continued to hold a privileged place in the life of the nation. First of all, in the physical sense, by its preponderance. The urban areas covered at most only a twentieth of the country's surface. Elsewhere the rural expanses prevailed, as the centre of traditional country life and ancestral influences. Wherever you went in England you found fields and pastures, peaceful flocks and large trees, endless hedges and earth roads, small villages and thatched farms. Such was the almost uniform pattern of the countryside. 'Nothing but green' was Taine's description. On the other hand the forests, despoiled in former times for naval construction, occupied very little space, and no effort was made to replant them.

The age-old traditions of rural civilization were also solidly entrenched in habits of thought and in social relations. Land ownership remained the prime source of authority, prestige and influence. In spite of the powerful intrusion of commercial and manufacturing capitalism from the eighteenth century onwards, it did not succeed in upsetting the old idea, dating from the origins of agrarian society, that land was the fundamental asset. So it followed that power should belong to the owners of the soil. Furthermore labour on the land was endowed with a thousand virtues and continued to symbolize labour in its purest form.

Everything was impregnated with the rural spirit – mentalities, ways of thought and language. Even the two main foundations of the national culture – classical antiquity for the educated élite and the Bible for all – helped to strengthen the primacy of the country. Biblical echoes and Virgilian tags commended the peace of the fields while they strengthened the conviction that there resided the true habitat of man. Not that it can have been very easy to compare the rubicund drovers of herds of short-horns to shepherds of Arcadia! But these bucolic impulses, brought up to date by capitalism and revitalized by agricultural science, came alive again by their association with progress and well-being. Furthermore, as people saw the enormous increase in yields arising from the agricultural revolution, how could they not marvel at the results which even the inhabitants of the Promised Land could not have imagined in their wildest dreams? And the prestige of the countryside was raised even further by 'the taste of the wealthiest and most influential section of the nation for rural life' which was noticed by the Frenchman Léonce de Lavergne, a great admirer of English agriculture.

In certain respects ruralism even gained ground instead of retreating. As industrial civilization tightened its grip, an ardent quest for nature began to develop, as a sort of defence reaction. People felt a growing need for the country as an antidote to the urban environment. Hence the love of greenery, of gardens and lawns. 'The town-dweller does all he can to cease being a town-dweller' observed Taine as early as 1860. And after that the process never ceased to gain strength, making a profound mark on town architecture and town life. In this superiority granted to the country over the town we see a sign of green England's resistance to the spread of black England, much more than a nostalgia for the past. The country, admitting a material defeat, took a spiritual revenge on the town by winning men's hearts.

It is certainly true that the population of the countryside began to diminish in a marked way. Not that the abolition of the Corn Laws in 1846 struck a fatal blow to agriculture. That is a legend that must be contradicted. Supported by favourable conditions, the working of the land successfully survived free trade; and the 'Victorian prosperity' from 1851 to 1873 benefited as much from agriculture as from industrial and commercial enterprise. Nevertheless the pull of the towns was stronger. Towards the middle of the nineteenth century the rural exodus began to take a new turn. Here and there losses in manpower occurred, for the departures outstripped the natural population growth. In his study of rural depopulation J. Saville has shown that it was in the 1851 census that for the first time purely agricultural counties (e.g. Wiltshire in England and Montgomeryshire in Wales) showed a drop in population.[29] In the following decades, the same tendency affected East Anglia, Cornwall and most of the Welsh counties. However, one must not exaggerate this tendency because, according to Bowley's estimates, in the second half of the nineteenth century, the total rural population went down by less than 10 per cent, having grown by 50 per cent in the first half.[30] So ritual lamentations on deserted villages should be greeted with some reserve. Nevertheless, even if in absolute figures the drop was slow, in relative terms the story was very different. In 1871 the proportion of the rural population to the urban population was exactly the reverse of what had obtained at the beginning of the century: one-third countrymen and two-thirds town-dwellers, as against two-thirds and one-third. The number of workers in agriculture, which was just over 2 million in 1851 dropped to 1.6 million in 1881, and their proportion in the total labour force fell between those two dates from one-fifth to one-eighth. (At the end of the eighteenth century it was two-fifths.) Even more marked was the retreat of agriculture within the economic activity of the country. From 1851 to 1881, with an equal turnover (rather more than £100 million) agriculture saw its contribution drop from one-fifth to one-tenth of the national income.

Yet rural society held its own. It kept its cohesion in a remarkable way. One of its characteristics was its homogeneity arising from a shared life in contact with nature and the land, and from the survival of semi-feudal traditions. Another was its fundamental variety, seeing that the rural community, made up of three layers, was divided into three blocks whose limits could not be crossed. In appearance there was nothing in common between a country gentleman – rich, civilized and treated with the respect that surrounded old families – and the poor illiterate day-labourer who toiled all day on the land. Yet they were bound together by a sense of solidarity that went far beyond patronage on one side and dependence on the other.

For the originality of the British countryside lay in the fact that a highly capitalist agriculture developed, without a break, within the framework of an earlier structure, that is to say the feudal and aristocratic system. This system, entrenched in its near-monopoly of the land and its alliance with the Church, managed to survive in many institutions and even more in modes of conduct, while adapting itself to the requirements of new methods of production. This explains the three-layer structure of rural society, each man in his own station, and the three levels defined with the utmost exactitude. It was thus a society characterized by a stable and rigid hierarchy with very little mobility indeed.

At the top of the pyramid were the landed capitalists, the owners of the soil. Aristocrats belonging to the peerage or the gentry, drawing most of their income from land rents, they lived in their manor, hall or country house, leaving the task of running their properties to their agent. In the centre of the hierarchy were the farmers who paid rent on their farms in exchange for a lease. Working their land made them both employers of labour and producers, and more or less members of the middle class. Finally, at the bottom of the social scale, was the world of hired farm-workers. Labourers, ploughmen, shepherds, farm servants and the like, they formed an agricultural proletariat, plentiful and submissive, generally very poor and exploited. These 'agricultural labourers', on

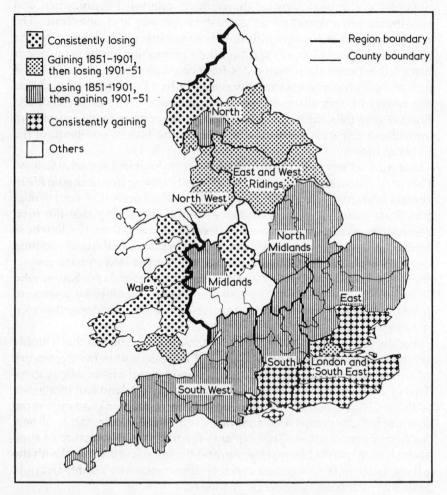

Map 3. Internal migration in England and Wales, 1851–1951[31]

whose efforts depended the working of the soil, were very often neg-
lected, if not actually ill-treated.

Let us consider the respective sizes of the three elements that made up
the rural world. One can reckon that in 1851 the landlords did not number
more than a few thousand. The tenant farmers, who rented their land,
amounted to a quarter of a million, while the wage-earners numbered
about 1,250,000 agricultural labourers. Two conclusions can be drawn
from this analysis. Firstly, the extreme simplicity of the social pyramid,
from the wide spread of the base up to the narrow point of the summit.
Secondly, one sees that the three levels of the social hierarchy faithfully
reproduce the fundamental division of English society into three classes:
aristocracy, middle class and manual workers.

Later on, in the detailed study of social stratification, we will find each
of these categories placed at its national level (see chaps 2 and 3).
However, to understand the rural world and its cohesive strength fully,
one would have to view at the same time the horizontal divisions – the trio
landlords/tenant farmers/labourers – and the vertical unity, the result of
the integrating powers of the old society of the soil. For the existence of a
rural community did not derive solely from a certain unity of interests
among all those who lived on the same land – in other words, the landed
interest. Tradition and style of life also counted. In fact, despite enormous
differences in income and standard of living, in power and culture, the
rural world felt itself united in its association with nature and the earth, by
the immemorial rhythm of the seasons and the days, and perhaps even
more by the weight of age-old customs, both of castle and of cottage ('The
rich man in his castle, the poor man at his gate'). Hence the common
acceptance of an order considered unchangeable and ordained by the
Creator, symbolized every Sunday in church by the squire and his family
in their own pew, the farmers in their comfortable decent seats, while the
labourers, crowded and standing, were relegated to the back of the aisle.

The preciseness of the social structures reflect the relative simplicity of
agrarian structures, in spite of regional differences. A country of large
estates and medium-sized farms is how one might summarize the situation in England in the second half of the nineteenth century. The enclos-
ures were just about at an end, for the simple reason that there was not
much left to enclose. On the contrary there was a reversal of the century-
old tendency after 1870, as shown in a new interest in the preservation of
common grounds. The 'commons', now considered as green open spaces
to be preserved, acquired a sudden importance, forerunners of the 'green
belts' and the special land reserves. In spite of this tentative effort, the
concentration of property, which had continued uninterrupted since the
eighteenth century, reached its peak around 1875–80. Certainly the small
independent farmer did not disappear entirely, but he was hard pressed

from all sides and only survived in patches, generally in the hilly regions like the Lake District, Devonshire, Wales and the marshy Fens. These 'yeomen', who inherited from freeholding forebears and worked the land themselves (they were the only people who could reasonably be called peasants) only held a very small portion of England's soil, from 12 to 15 per cent.

We are fairly well informed on the ownership of landed property at that time thanks to an inquiry carried out on the orders of Parliament in 1873. This document, nicknamed the 'New Domesday Book' after the famous land register set up by William the Conqueror, was in effect the first official survey of land distribution to be carried out since 1086. It came into existence because evidence was required to refute attacks regularly mounted by the Radicals. They took up the arguments developed at length by the free traders and the Chartists in the 1840s and denounced the aristocratic monopoly of land ownership. In the event, the evidence of the inquiry, far from refuting these attacks, revealed a much higher degree of concentration than had been thought, and brought grist to the mill of the enemies of aristocracy and privilege. Shortly afterwards Joseph Chamberlain was to launch his famous attack on idle landowners who 'toil not neither do they spin'. In fact the extraordinary power and wealth of the landlords shows up with blinding clarity, however one presents the figures. Four-fifths of the soil of the United Kingdom belonged to less than 7,000 people, and the owners of more than 1,000 acres held two-thirds of the land under cultivation in Great Britain.[32] In England and Wales half the land was in the hands of 4,200 owners, while one quarter belonged to 360 magnates whose domains extended to more than 10,000 acres each. In Scotland, the concentration was even greater since 24 owners possessed between them a quarter of the country, with one estate passing the fabulous figure of one million acres, and 350 individuals shared two-thirds of the soil.[33] It was not possible for smallholders, although they numbered a million, with patches often not larger than a pocket handkerchief, to counterbalance the power concentrated in the hands of the minority of landlords. So everywhere the great estates dominated without rival.

A very different situation obtained for the size of farms. Usually the great estates were broken up into farms of modest size, all the more because the richest landlords rarely owned continuous stretches of land. Indeed their estates often spread over several counties. In 1851, out of a total of 215,000 farms, the small units were the most numerous, 90,000 being of between 5 and 20 acres; but one should note that they only covered 8.6 per cent of the area under cultivation. It is true, on the other hand, that their number tended to grow. In the twenty-five years following they almost doubled, but without occupying more than 14 or 15 per cent of the total. The first place was occupied by medium-sized farms. There were 45,000 farms of 50–100 acres, occupying 13 per cent, and 54,000 farms of 100–300 acres occupying 45 per cent of the total surface. This category remained pretty stable, and still occupied three-fifths of the land under cultivation at the end of the century. Finally large farms, the favourite scene for 'high farming', made up a very important proportion, i.e. one third of the total surface in 1851, with 12,000 farms of 300–500 acres covering 17.5 per cent, 4,000 farms of 500–1,000 acres covering 11.5 per cent and nearly 800 farms of more than 1,000 acres covering 5 per cent of the total surface. In 1885, large farms continued to account for nearly 30 per cent of all cultivated land.[34]

During the wave of prosperity which lasted from 1851 to 1873, equipment and methods of farming were gradually modernized. There was an effort to put into practice the maxim laid down by the great agronomist and recognized authority, Caird: 'High farming – the best substitute for Protection'.[35] One sign of prosperity was the rise in estate revenue and the land values. Rents, already rising since 1835, continued to increase until 1879. The rise was between 25 and 45 per cent, according to the region. For producers, whether tenant farmers or landowners, this resulted in high profits. The lot of the labourers, on the other hand, hardly changed at all.

The growth of demand at home both stimulated and diversified production. A line of demarcation continued to separate the England of cereal crops to the east and south, consisting mostly of wheat, from the England of pasture lands to the west and south-west; but meadow lands and cattle-breeding never ceased to make headway. Around 1870, 43 per cent of all agricultural land consisted of grass and, out of the ploughland making up the rest, one third was taken up with artificial pastures and root crops for forage. On the other hand rural craftsmen suffered severely from the competition of mechanized industry. A village carpenter, victim of the slump, complained that, 'But for the coffins, he would starve!'[36] And yet the world of the village, sheltered and peaceful, with its traditional patterns, retained its way of life without being too shaken by contemporary material change.

Material civilization: the dividends of progress

The English might freely recognize the superiority of their French rivals in matters of artistic refinement, manners, fashion and gastronomy, but they were justified in claiming for themselves the role of pioneers in all that concerned practical life and the open air. Indeed they were responsible for two inventions that were to spread throughout Europe – domestic comfort and sport. As Rimbaud wrote:

Ce sont les conquérants du monde. . . .
Le sport et le confort voyagent avec eux.[37]

In this area innovation generally started in high society. The middle classes imitated it until eventually, with the lapse of time and with the requisite standard of living, it reached the less privileged. In society, remarked a Victorian, ideas rise upwards from below, while manners descend from above. Some of the innovations, however, were so important in themselves that they turned everyone's habits upside down at once. This was true of railways which, in revolutionizing travel, transformed people's existence. Who could refuse the advantages of speed, in spite of some discomfort in the third class? The number of passengers rose from 5 million in 1838 to 54 million ten years later. In 1854 it passed 100 million; in 1869 it reached 300 million and, in 1876, 517 million.[38] The change occurred without a transitional period. At one blow the old methods of transport were abandoned. In 1841 a journey by coach from London to Exeter took 18 hours; after 1845 it took $6\frac{1}{2}$ hours by express train. At the same time the fare for the journey went down from £4 to £2 10s. first class.

Towards 1860–70 the existence of railways began to produce a profound change in living habits. Until then a suburban residence had been the privilege of a very few well-to-do people, owners of a carriage and pair. Now the number and frequency of suburban trains allowed many prosperous bourgeois to live far from their work in comfortable houses away from the smoke, the noise and the turmoil of the centre. When they began the English suburbs were a preserve of the rich, and so conferred social prestige on their inhabitants.

The railway did not, however, only serve the daily commuters. It also transformed leisure. From the middle of the century onwards excursions to the seaside became more and more frequent. Excursion trains poured out hordes of day-trippers onto the beaches of Margate, Gravesend and Brighton. Other longer journeys took Englishmen onto the Continent in growing numbers. Thomas Cook started his business in 1845 and towards 1870 his name became a household word. In 1857 the Alpine Club was founded, and the number of climbers increased rapidly, combining sport with travel. Winter holidays in the South of France became fashionable, and Queen Victoria helped to launch the Côte d'Azur by her visits there. Other travellers crossed the oceans, and Jules Verne paid a deserved tribute to the British in making Phileas Fogg in Round the World in Eighty Days the model of the intrepid and determined globe-trotter.

In domestic life the middle classes did their best to combine utility with comfort. In that bourgeois age there was more concern for usefulness than elegance. Everything solid and practical was appreciated. It was the heyday of large comfortable armchairs, sofas and ottomans. Mass production turned out thousands of pieces of furniture, washing facilities and household utensils. As a sign of the desire for comfort and visible wealth, one found in homes a profusion of curtains, draperies, carpets, hangings, pouffes, lamps, overmantels, etc. The habit of taking baths became general. This usually meant a tub into which hot or cold water was poured. Frequent cold baths were recommended for hardening children, starting with the most delicate. About 1865 the daily bath became a habit in high society, the middle classes being satisfied with one a week. As for bathrooms, they did not appear until the end of the century, but the flushing water closet became general after 1850.

A mass of minor innovations contributed to the change in lifestyle, easing and simplifying the daily round. In 1840 the modern postal system was created with the introduction of a stamp paid for by the sender – the 'Penny Post'. The number of letters sent quadrupled in ten years. At about the same time the steel nib replaced the goose quill, and blotting paper replaced sand. People started to use 'little sacks of paper, called envelopes' instead of sealing folds with wax. Matches of sulphur or phosphorus (they were called 'lucifers' or 'prometheans') took the place of tinder-boxes, and in 1845 Browning's poem *Meeting at Night* celebrated the new invention, which was already in general use:

> . . . the quick sharp scratch
> And blue spurt of a lighted match

Other innovations which transformed material life around 1840–50 were cheap soap, sewing machines, and gasoline for lamps instead of colza oil. Cigarettes were introduced by English soldiers returning from the Crimea, where they had acquired the habit from their French comrades-in-arms. However the smoking-room, the area dedicated to the pleasure of tobacco, did not make its appearance until the last third of the century. Then it became the rule.

Food consumption increased among the middle classes and, to a certain extent, among the working classes. Treatises on domestic economy became widespread, from the culinary advice given by a French chef, Soyer, who through his good reputation was given the job of catering for the 1851 Exhibition, to the classic *Household Management* by Mrs Beeton, published in 1861 and endlessly reprinted. The habit of copious breakfasts consisting of tea, toast, eggs, fish, ham, etc. became established. Even among workmen breakfast was far from negligible. Afternoon tea was a Victorian novelty. Launched by the Duchess of Bedford, it won over the aristocracy and from there spread among the bourgeoisie in the middle of the century. Consumption of food by the masses did not grow during the first half of the nineteenth century, but prosperity after 1850 brought rapid improvement. The annual consumption of sugar per person rose from 18 lbs at Victoria's accession to 54 lbs in 1870–9, and tea from 1½ lbs to 4¼ lbs. As for beer every Englishman drank an average of 20 gallons (90 litres) a year around 1830; fifty years later he drank 36 gallons (165 litres). Consumption of tobacco also increased between those dates, going up from 14 ozs to 1½ lbs (375 to 630 grams) per person.[39]

In a country which was covered by more and more houses, streets and smoke, urban life made physical exercise almost a necessity. The need for recreation in the open air became imperative. Up till then such sports as had existed had reflected the spirit of rural civilization, whence they sprang. They were generally violent and involved the rearing and killing of animals. In aristocratic circles the traditional pastimes were shooting, fox-hunting, fishing and especially horse-racing, which had the additional lure of gambling. There were the classic races like the Derby, the St Leger, Ascot and, after 1839, the Grand National. The working classes entertained themselves with sports that were equally violent – wrestling, boxing, and above all fights between animals, e.g. cocks, dogs and rats, and bull-baiting.

Towards the middle of the nineteenth century, under the influence of the public schools, team games appeared which provided exciting recreation for the spirit as well as the body. The fashion was now for refined games controlled by rules. The idea was to take exercise that was beneficial in its appeal to endurance, team spirit and manly qualities. Sport became a school for character. Its association with making money was frowned on, and one played for pleasure and not for the betting. In matches it was the sense of competition and fair play that were important. Submission to rules was felt to have moral and disciplinary value, and there was the additional advantage that a larger number of people could take part in refreshing exercise.

Social divisions were as clearly marked out in these new sports as they were in the old. Among the gentleman's games were cricket, an ancient game that now acquired great prestige (even giving rise to the expression 'it's not cricket'), rugby football, first played at Rugby School (the Rugby Union was founded in 1871), golf, imported from Scotland in 1869 (whence its name 'Scotch golf'), rowing (the Oxford and Cambridge Boat Race became an annual event around 1856), and polo around 1870. Athletics started at Oxford in about 1850. Croquet became fashionable at the same date. As for lawn tennis, it was invented in 1874 and codified shortly afterwards by the Wimbledon All England Croquet and Lawn Tennis Club. By the end of the century tennis and bicycling had become the great recreations of the middle classes.

The favourite game of the working classes was association football or 'soccer' which quickly outstripped 'rugger' in popularity. The Football

One might note at this point that the noun 'unemployed' and the word 'unemployment' made their first appearances in the Oxford English Dictionary in 1882 and 1888 respectively.

By the same token the long-vaunted merits of competition became suspect. Wasn't it just this unlimited competition that led inexorably to the crushing of the feeble? Where people used to gorge themselves on Social Darwinism, applying, after Spencer, the 'struggle for life' notion to business so as to justify the selection of the stronger and the disappearance of the less able, opinion now went abruptly into reverse. It was seen that such arguments for a hierarchy, quoting 'natural law', resulted in unfairness. All these discoveries dealt severe blows to *laissez-faire*.

There was a parallel change of view on the other great question of the day, pauperism and its causes. Up to then there had been the constant refrain, based on the teachings of the classical economists, that each person in society met with the fate he deserved. Now it was precisely this subordination of economic to moral considerations that was put in question. The prime explanation of poverty (the argument now ran) must not be sought in the personal failings of the individual as orthodox individualism asserted, but in the disorder of the markets and their corollary, an unjust society. It was a bold assertion, even scandalous, but was corroborated by the facts patiently revealed by the social surveys. An important discovery, and for many a revelation. What were the causes of poverty? They did not reside, as had been thought, in laziness, improvidence, drink, promiscuousness and vice among the 'lower classes'. Poverty resulted above all from the malfunctioning of an industrial system which did not assure workers either regular employment or decent wages. It only too often condemned the man to forced idleness, the woman to prostitution and the child to the slums. Consequently the key to balanced happiness must be sought in the economic order rather than in individual morality. Instead of a moral debate with a subjective and individualistic ethos, there were now ideas abroad that blamed the structures. It was now up to society to take the welfare of its members in hand by making the necessary changes.

What a long road had been travelled since the middle of the century! What a reversal of ideas! In the old days optimism reigned supreme, carried along by that fine utilitarian confidence in 'the March of Intellect'. It was the time when the Crystal Palace was the symbol of economic success, material progress and the mastery of man over the machine; when Thomas Arnold saluted ecstatically the advent of the railway, thinking that he had seen signs that 'feudalism had disappeared for ever'. Now here was his son, the great Matthew Arnold, being the first to denounce the mechanical and joyless existence of the inhabitants of large towns, the hollowness of a progress that had brought with it only materialism and philistinism. In a sarcastic observation which has an astonishingly modern ring he asserted, a century ahead of our time, that for the bourgeois of his day it was the acme of civilization that trains ran every quarter of an hour between Islington and Camberwell, and that there were twelve deliveries of post a day between the same districts. But what was the good of all that if it only enabled people to pass from a dull and limited life in Islington to an equally dull and insipid life in Camberwell and if the letters only proved that the writers had nothing to say to each other?[7]

Pessimism and anxiety became the rule. The men of the late-Victorian and Edwardian generations freely admitted that they were 'in the dark' and that 'the unknown' surrounded them. And yet, someone will say, wasn't this the moment when imperialism was at its most successful? How could so many conquests by the Anglo-Saxon race fail to restore the nation's optimism? In fact questionings and uncertainties still persisted. One finds them right up to the great *Recessional* of Rudyard Kipling written for the 1897 Jubilee. Some hoped to exorcize their fears for the future by repeated self-disparagement, as in that masterpiece of economic masochism, the celebrated pamphlet *Made in Germany* which appeared in 1896, or by imagining some impending apocalypse. 'We are uncertain whether civilization is about to blossom into flower or wither in a ruined tangle of dead leaves and faded gold.'[8] However most thinking people chose the way of lucid thought, without illusion or pretence. It was this determination to see clearly, so as to arrive at a rational view of the world, away from traditional taboos, that was perfectly expressed by the economist J. A. Hobson when he wrote in *The Crisis of Liberalism* (1909) that more and more people were 'possessed by the duty and the desire to put the very questions which their parents felt shocking, and to insist upon plain intelligible answers.'[9]

So the intellectual foundations of *laissez-faire* were beginning to totter, even though the doctrine retained a great number of adherents. It would indeed be entirely wrong to underestimate the imprint of economic individualism, whose influence on the public mind can be traced up to our own times. Yet new ideological currents were infiltrating through all the cracks in the liberal edifice. They all led to a redefinition of the relationship between the State and the individual. They all carried England towards a restoration of the functions and the power of the State, either in the limited framework of interventionism (the radical way) or by advocating nationalization and collective management (the socialist way). So one sees why an ultra-individualist like Dicey did not hesitate to name 1870 as the last year of English liberalism, for he saw it as the beginning of Moloch State's takeover of public life. With more subtlety Elie Halévy decided to put later, in the last years of the century, the decisive turning-point of modern England, i.e. the decline of liberal individualism inspired by Protestantism and the advent of a Prussian and bureaucratic conception of the State. Indeed he foresaw it as a dangerous prelude to the 'era of tyrannies'.

In practice, the radicalism, rejuvenated and refreshed, which governed England from 1906 to 1914, took upon itself the mission of combining the virtues of individualism and private enterprise with the government intervention necessary to correct abuses and protect the rights of the weakest. This was a difficult gamble, and while political democracy gained from it, capitalism was hardly inconvenienced. As for socialism, another gainer from the crisis of classical liberalism, it usually emerged as the winner of ideological encounters. This was firstly because it brought an answer to the age's double yearning for rationalism and justice. Secondly, within a few years, it succeeded in capturing the attention and sometimes the support of the intelligentsia. One might even describe the period as the golden age of English socialism. After the 1914 war, Labour's progress was electoral and political, but the doctrinal inspiration dried up; whereas between 1880 and 1914 the current of socialism was in full spate. There was Marxist socialism, with the Social-Democratic Federation, founded in 1884, as its main support; there was Fabian socialism, the Fabian Society having also been founded in 1884; and there was religious socialism, as the Christian socialism of 1848 had a vigorous revival at the end of the century. On the labour side there was the Independent Labour Party, created in 1893, which acted as a link between the advanced wing of trade unionism and the elements of the middle class won over to the liberation of the workers; and there was revolutionary 'syndicalism' whose forceful thrusts began in 1910.

Traditional beliefs and new modes of behaviour

Should one take Virginia Woolf literally when she claimed that 'in or about December 1910 human character changed'. For in that year, according to her, 'all human relations have shifted – those between masters and servants, husbands and wives, parents and children. And when human relations change there is at the same time a change in religion, conduct, politics and literature.'[10] Of course it was a case of the contemporary observer's imagination wanting at all costs to assign a date to the changes in civilization unrolling before her eyes. But equally there was a profound intuition at work. Hers was a mind seeking to penetrate the tendencies of her own times, to take their measure and fix landmarks. It is true that the dawn of the new century brought so many changes in material existence, in manners and in mental outlook that the old society was stirred by a thousand new ideas and ambitions. Cheap newspapers, bicycles and motor cars, mass leisure for the first time, changes in dress fashion, *fin de siècle* aestheticism, 'Edwardian' decor, how could all these innovations fail to make people feel that they were entering a new world? – even though there still remained the vast weight of inertia in a society where tradition was credited as a major virtue, and where new ideas came up against formidable obstacles. 'In England', remarked Sidney Webb wittily, 'there are three stages through which every notion has to pass: 1. It is impossible; 2. It is against the Bible; 3. We knew it before.'[11]

However, once the size of the change has been underlined, rather than taking a bird's eye view of the many manifestations of the 'new spirit', we prefer to concentrate our analysis on two sectors: religion and the family. These are special areas that control social conduct at a deep level, but they are hard to penetrate in spite of much research, for they are sealed up by secrets buried in individual consciences or in the collective unconscious. Nevertheless two pieces of evidence jump to the eye – the retreat of religious faith and the drop in the birth-rate. It is this decisive change in behaviour, making a complete break with the habits of centuries, that we must study here.

We have already seen to what degree England was a Christian country and how its history and outlook were conditioned by the various religious sects. Whether he liked it or not, every Englishman was moulded by Christianity to the depths of his being. Of course one must not idealize the situation. The existence of active centres of free thought, the de-christianization of the common people, the more or less open resistance to the established Church's continuous presence were obvious and long-standing facts whose origins went back beyond the mid-century. The new development at the end of the Victorian period and even more in the first years of the twentieth century was the gradual disruption of the traditional balance between religion and society. This retreat took three forms. First of all there was the retreat of the Churches as institutions directing and controlling everybody's life. In fact the Christian world began to disappear. In the world that succeeded it the profane and the sacred coexisted in peace, but without the former being, as before, subordinate to the latter. Secondly faith, insofar as it was a personal belief and a source of interior life, tended to become a minority phenomenon because of the gradual decline of traditional Christianity. The latter faded away and was replaced by smaller religious communities that were far less numerous but generally more convinced and fervent. Finally, as Christianity exercised less and less social influence, religion gradually lost its important role as a cohesive force in the community.

One can see clearly that there was a process at work going far beyond the ritual lamentations over the disintegrating effect of rationalism, the vogue of science, the irruption of hedonism and materialism, and the taste for comfort and leisure pursuits. Undoubtedly all these factors counted, but should we call them causes or merely contributors to a process?

In this general decline it was obviously the Church of England that was most affected. Her position as the official Church probably did her more harm than good in her efforts to spread the Gospel and carry out good works. The churches were half empty, and the recruitment of clergy was not without difficulty, all the more because the livings were affected by the agricultural crisis. In the country the vicarage was no better-off than the manor. The situation in the towns, where enormous efforts had been made to establish new parishes, settled down more or less. The distribution of charity and the festive character of religious ceremonies helped to keep congregations in existence round the clergyman. However, on the eve of the First World War, the total number of Easter communicants was only 2.2 million, or 10 per cent of the population over 15 years old. The situation was not much better on the Nonconformist side. After the peak years 1870–80, a slow decline in attendance at the chapels took place. A loss of vitality, the disappearance of the old urban congregations as the middle classes moved to the suburbs, the weakening of the Liberal party, the scarcity of ministers – all these debilitating factors were outweighed by the efforts towards re-union made by various sects.

Another disturbing symptom for the Protestants was that no more 'revivals' occurred after the middle of the nineteenth century. The Oxford Movement was the last of the great religious awakenings. One could hardly consider ritualism, salvationism (the Salvation Army dated from 1865–78) or, in the Methodist Church, the Forward Movement, as anything but pale successors. There were other small but revealing signs of changes in religious attitudes. Family prayers in the morning, with the children and servants present, were gradually discontinued with the aristocracy showing the way. There was less observance of Sunday. For example the National Sunday League organized railway excursions at low prices; and in 1896 a law authorized the Sunday opening of museums, to the great outrage of the traditionalists. Still the famous English sabbath justly maintained its reputation as an austere day which was only cheered a little for the working classes by the pub and the Sunday roast-beef.

All the statistics on religious practice agree in showing up the indifference of a large proportion of the people. This holds true even when one takes into account the uncertainty of the criteria of church membership that reflected the bourgeoisie's and clergy's view of religion. For instance in Sheffield an inquiry carried out in 1881 fully bore out the conclusions of the religious census of 1851 – only one out of three who could and should have been practising Christians attended church. In London a survey conducted by the *Daily News* in 1903 arrived at a similar result: church-

goers amounted to between one-fifth and one-sixth of the total population. On the eve of the war, only three marriages out of four were
celebrated in church in England and Wales. In Scotland, on the other
hand, the proportion of religious marriages was still about nine out of
ten.[13] The only denomination to increase their numbers were the Roman
Catholics. In 1900 there were about 2 million in Great Britain, of whom
more than 400,000 were in Scotland; and in 1914 they formed 5 per cent of
the population in England and 11 per cent in Scotland. By comparison the
Methodists numbered 750,000; the Baptists and Congregationalists oscil-
lated around 400,000 members each; and the total number of Presbyterians came to 1.2 million, nearly all concentrated in Scotland.[14] As for
the Church of England statistics, they varied in the proportion of seven to
one, depending on whether one counted all the nominal members of the
Church of England or only the Easter communicants. Finally, if one lays
on one side Roman Catholicism (which was on the increase) and posi-
tively declared atheism (which was very rare) on the other, it was indif-
ferentism which was becoming more and more common. Behind a façade
of religious institutions and traditional customs, England was becoming
secularized, in the personal as well as in the public sphere; but there still
remained, even among the indifferent, a sense of the sacred and puritan

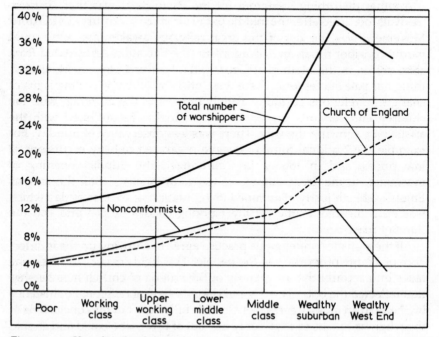

Figure 2.   Church attendance among adults by social class in London at the
beginning of the twentieth century[12]

morality. Above all there was everpresent an undenominational religious outlook.

At the same time an important turning-point was reached in family life – the start of voluntary birth-control. The practice itself was not new. What was new was its practice on a vast scale. One can fix the date exactly; it started some time around 1875–80 and in a few years reached massive proportions, changing the whole demographic face of England. Just as the French had done a few decades earlier and as other European nations would soon do, the English broke with ancestral habits and adopted new modes of behaviour in human reproduction. These led not only to a change of attitude towards children, but also to a new conception of the family and life in general.

We must distinguish here two aspects of this upset of traditional ways. First of all simple facts, and here the picture is as clear as daylight. Then there is the interpretation of these facts, and we start to stumble in the dark. We will begin by letting the figures speak for themselves. They describe a curve of extreme simplicity on the demographic graph. Firstly the birth-rate, which had been nearly stable for half a century at around 35 per 'ooo, diminished from 1875–80, then dived steeply to end up at 24 per 'ooo, in the years just before 1914. Secondly, the net reproduction rate naturally followed the same pattern, i.e. having wavered between 1.4 and 1.5 between 1851 and 1871, it fell in 1911 to 1.1, only just achieving replacement between generations. The third criterion, which was even more revealing, was the number of children per family. Around 1870 it was 6; in 1890–9 it dropped to 4.3, and in 1915 it was no more than 2.3.

It was an extraordinary decline in fertility, and a very sudden one too, concentrated into a very short time. The transformation occurred within thirty years, or a generation. How does one explain a mutation of this magnitude? It is worth noting that, although the drop in the birth-rate affected all classes eventually, it started with the ruling classes. It was the bourgeoisie, and in particular the professions who started the trend, whereas the tendency was less striking and certainly slower to develop among urban manual workers and agricultural labourers. In fact recent demographic research has shown that the process had already started in certain groups at the beginning of the nineteenth century, in the aristocracy for example. Average figures should not mask the differences that existed between social classes. The differences are glaring when one starts to calculate fertility by socio-economic groups, the proportion approaching two to one. For couples married in the period 1890–9 the average number of children per family in the professions was 2.80, among the salaried employees (white-collar workers) 3.04, among the manual wage-earners 4.85, and among the labourers 5.11. For couples married in

1914 the figures had everywhere diminished but the proportions were much the same:

Professional   2.05
Salaried employees   1.95
Manual wage-earners   3.24
Labourers   4.09[15]

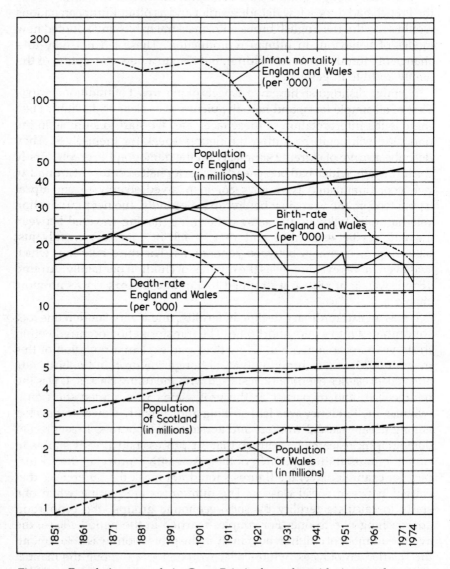

Figure 3. Populations trends in Great Britain from the mid-nineteenth century

As a result of these statistics eugenics started to flourish as a theory under the pretext of preventing the increase of unhealthy stock and improving the biological and mental quality of the race – so widespread was the fear of seeing England deprived of its élite and becoming a country dominated numerically by the degenerate and alcoholic 'lower classes'.

So one point is established, that the spread of new methods of birth-control through English society started from the top. It was the upper classes who were the first to restrain their fertility. It was their example and the pressure of the cultural model embodied by them that gradually imposed a norm of one or two children per family. But if one searches more closely for the motivations of a transformation that was so funda-mental, one comes up against problems with no clear answer, so that one has to guess rather than offer clear-cut replies. Would one support, for example, Bagehot and Spencer by saying that the diversification of leisure and pastimes diminished the role of sexuality and so reduced procrea-tion?[16] Shouldn't one rather invoke material considerations, improved living standards, the desire for more comfort, the fears of the bourgeoisie in face of the 'great depression' and the uncertainties of the future – all factors which would lead to the limiting of numbers so as to draw more profit from existing resources? Oughtn't one also to adduce the new ideas about children's futures, the wider ambitions of parents for their off-spring, the worries about education and, above all, about 'getting on'? All these trends required that care be concentrated on smaller numbers so as to ensure success in the race for promotion, especially as social mobility, although loudly proclaimed, was in fact fairly limited. Similarly, did the progress of education and labour legislation have its effect, delaying entry into the world of production, while the cost of bringing up children tended to rise? How can one measure the fading of that age-old fatalism, which meant that all children were accepted passively as 'sent by God'? And what was the impact of a neo-Malthusianism (heralded by the resounding Bradlaugh-Besant case in 1877) which preached birth-control in the name of the struggle against poverty and overpopulation? All these factors certainly played their part. But were they decisive?

On the other hand we must reject two explanations often advanced, on the grounds that they affected the situation only much later. It is undeni-able that the factors involved accelerated the process at a later stage, but they did not have much effect at the beginning. The first was women's desire for emancipation. The desire to be freed from the slavery of mater-nity was indeed felt, but it always held a secondary place in that period, as the works of J. and O. Banks have shown. Furthermore feminist aspira-tions only began to be a force after 1900. The other explanation was the spread of contraceptive techniques. In spite of progress in the manufacture of contraceptives and spermicides, the methods used remained extremely rudimentary. The fall in the birth-rate was above all attributable to *coitus interruptus*, while the more refined methods of contraception were the preserve of a small minority even among the educated classes. It followed that birth-control remained for some time a male prerogative.

One last point remains to be emphasized, which does not seem to have had enough attention. Parallel with the drop in the birth-rate, a continuous and very marked drop in the death-rate was evident in the last quarter of the nineteenth century. This had been very stable from 1850 to 1875 at around 22 per '000, but it decreased steadily after that period to arrive at 14 per '000 in 1901–13. This change was due to two main causes: improvement in nutrition and progress in hygiene. On the other hand, infant mortality played no part in this decline, except right at the end of the period, for it remained at the constant and very high level of 15 per '000 right up to 1900. As the adult mortality declined, the difference between births and deaths remained constant, even though fertility diminished. As natural growth, and so the future of the nation, seemed assured, why shouldn't families from now onwards indulge their new ambitions and control their fertility, a policy which seemed to guarantee a better life for all, both parents and children? Such a new demographic regulating system would explain how the transmission of life became dependent on the new mechanism of voluntary fertility instead of on the age-old drive of biological fertility.

Women make themselves heard

A new figure, presaging far greater upheavals, entered on the scene in the *fin de siècle* atmosphere when 'art nouveau', 'the new theatre' and 'the new realism' were making headway – 'the new woman'. Appearing soon after 1880, she dominated the 1890s and then consolidated her advance during the whole of the Edwardian period. She objected to the traditional balance of the sexes in terms that were sometimes moderate and more often radical, and she demanded a new definition of the sex roles. It was the beginning of the feminine revolt against the traditional order, the first steps on the long road to emancipation which has continued up to our own time. It was the harbinger of the 'sexual revolution' of the twentieth century.

Not that the struggle against 'sexism' had to wait for the end of the Victorian era to take shape. There had been a number of forerunners like Mary Wollstonecraft, the first of them all (*A Vindication of the Rights of Women*, 1792) and Barbara (Leigh Smith) Bodichon (*A Brief Summary of the Most Important Laws Concerning Women*, 1855). There were male champions of the equality of the sexes such as the socialist William Thompson (*Appeal of One Half of the Human Race*, 1825) and John Stuart Mill (*The Subjection of Women*, 1869). But they were voices crying in the wilderness, if one excludes certain isolated circles of convinced supporters. There were some remarkable individuals, victims of the inferiority of their sex, such as Harriet Martineau, Jane Carlyle, Harriet Taylor, Florence Nightingale etc., who had risen in protest against the oppressive tyranny under which they were suffering. In spite of all this it was not until the last quarter of the century that these feminist ideas gained ground and spread widely, thanks to some sudden publicity. Isolated efforts began to be coordinated and a real movement was born. In the face of enormous resistance it reached wider circles after 1900 in the upper and middle classes, and even in part of the working class.

Two traits of English feminism were apparent in this first phase of the struggle. Firstly its origin was bourgeois. It was amongst the privileged that the first stirrings were felt. As Viola Klein put it, feminism did not start in the factories, nor down the mines, but in middle-class Victorian drawing-rooms. At the start there was the activity of small intellectual groups with literary or political leanings, sometimes radical and sometimes socialist. In the next stage, as the battle was joined, a split began to appear between the moderates and the extremists. The latter inclined to total emancipation, including sexual liberty, while the former demanded first of all civil and political rights, without in the least putting in question the foundations of traditional morality. It was this second current of opinion that dominated English feminism in our period, showing the preponderance of the middle classes who were guided by a strict puritanism, by principles of duty and discipline, family loyalty, and a respectability imbued with the influence of religion. So the Rev. Hugh Price Hughes, the 'conscience of Wesleyanism', could congratulate himself in the first years of the twentieth century that the strictness of Protestantism had imprinted on British feminism a moral austerity that would protect it against the more dangerous aspects of Continental feminism . . . .[17]

To understand the revolt of the feminist *avant-garde* against the male order we must first of all give a brief sketch of the position of women in England during the second half of the nineteenth century, as well as examine the predominance of inegalitarian beliefs still held by the general public. We can then arrive at the methods, aims and progress of the fight for emancipation.

The feminine condition in the Victorian age derived from the existence of two superimposed structures – the ancient patriarchal regime and the modern bourgeois regime. Traditionally relations between the sexes were governed by a fundamental principle, the subordination of woman to man. This was the deep-rooted heritage of the age-old division of produc-

Empire on which the sun never set, there was many a household on which it never rose.

The harshness of social inequality had its roots in history. The great void that separated rich and poor was enormously enhanced by the rigidity of social attitudes, to such a degree that the gulf between the 'respectable' favourite of fortune and the manual worker was as deep subjectively as it was in fact. It was based on an inflexible class system, of which there were constant reminders in daily life. In London, for instance, at the entrance to public baths one might read: 'Workmen's baths; cold, 1 penny; hot, 3 pence. Others; cold, 3 pence; hot, 6 pence.' One has only to read the novels of Galsworthy or E. M. Forster to realize the multifarious nature of class distinctions. They could be seen everywhere, in modes of life, clothing and culture. Even physically the differences were striking. On the eve of the First World War, Oxford and Cambridge undergraduates were on average 3.25 inches taller and 25 pounds heavier than the working-class youths from the industrial areas of the Midlands and Lancashire, who were to be conscripted into the army three years later. In the period 1900–10 children in state schools aged 13 weighed on average 6.5 pounds more than children working in factories eighty years earlier. But children of the same age at 'public' schools were 2 to 3 ins taller than the children of agricultural workers. By the outbreak of the Second World War the difference had been reduced by half.[12] The difference in mortality is the most striking. In 1911, infant mortality was 76.4 per thousand in the middle and upper classes; the average for wage-earners was 132.5 per thousand, while for manual workers it was 152 per thousand and for miners 160 per thousand.[13]

Riches and Poverty, Leo Chiozza Money's book, published in 1905, provided some startling facts on the distribution of wealth, confirmed by later statisticians such as Bowley. Dealing with incomes, he drew a line, which he called the 'equator', dividing the British national product into two equal halves. But one half was shared out among 39 million people, while the remaining 5.5 million (12 per cent of the population) shared the whole of the other half of the cake. Ownership of capital was even more disproportionate, since Money showed that 120,000 people (amounting with their families to one-seventh of the population) owned two-thirds of the national capital – a mere handful of individuals with a monopoly of wealth. Extending his research to inheritances (although one-third escaped all or some tax, either through clever financial arrangements, or by fraud) he calculated that the 650,000 poorer people who died each year left bequests totalling £30 million, while fortunes amounting to £260 million were left by the 30,000 well-to-do (of whom 26 alone left property worth the total of that left by the poorer section).[14]

The breakdown of class was roughly as follows: upper class 5 per cent, middle class 15 per cent, lower class 80 per cent. In 1911 the labour force comprised 15 million manual workers (craftsmen, factory hands, labourers, domestic servants, farmworkers, transport workers); the lower middle class included 1.2 million clerks and other office workers, an equal number of tradesmen and shopkeepers, and the greater part of a total of 600,000 employers. In the middle class were to be found the remainder of the employers, businessmen, some tens of thousands of farmers and 400,000 members of the professions, civil servants, directors and managers.

Within the workers' world there were still two levels. The craftsman was far above the ordinary labourer; 'comfortable', 'self-respecting', he earned twice as much. For the proportion of unskilled labour among wage-earners was far higher than it was to be twenty or thirty years later. They formed a large impoverished group suffering all the uncertainties of the labour market. But for wage-earners as a whole the age of Edwardian prosperity meant stagnation and a fall in their standard of living. Between 1900 and 1913 there was no increase in the amount of goods and services consumed by the masses (moreover in this period there was a burst of emigration, 2.5 million people leaving the shores of Great Britain) whereas among the privileged there was glaring evidence of increase in income and well-being. Thus class differences were accentuated. The rich grew richer; the poor stagnated.

To get an idea of popular consumption before 1914 one need only look at an average working-class budget. A typical family of five or six lived on 45 shillings a week (including any possible earnings of wife or children). Of this sum almost half was spent on food; that is 33 pounds of bread and flour, 15.5 pounds of potatoes, 9 pounds of meat and bacon, two pounds of butter and margarine, 5.5 pounds of sugar, a dozen eggs, 9 pints of milk, 0.5 pound of tea, hardly any fruit or vegetables, very little fish, coffee or chocolate. Housing costs (rent, heat, lighting) amounted to 7 or 8 shillings. Seventeen shillings was all that was left for clothing, repairs, beer and tobacco, travel insurance payments, outings and family amusements. In fact the smallest accident could be enough to tip a family over the poverty line. No wonder this was the age of the public house. Wasn't drink the easiest, the most universally accessible way to forget, to escape from grinding poverty, gloomy streets and squalid housing? Beer consumption, on the increase ever since the earliest days of Queen Victoria, reached a record figure at the end of the century – about 3 pints a day per adult male.

Class differences were nothing new. What was new was the increased and lively recognition of their scale and their injustice; and this is what gave social conflict, arising out of labour unrest, its bitter character on both sides of the fence.

Education and class

The historian is faced with three different ways of looking at the history of education in England and its integration into the social structure. One way is to look at its long-term evolution and show how the country moved from a period of wholly private initiative, prior to Forster's Education Act of 1870, to one of public provision. The latter policy, looming up at the turn of the century, has become the accepted way ever since the Second World War. Between these utterly opposed systems – private versus public, local institution versus centralized control, spontaneous versus planned – there has never been war to the death. Accomodation has always been the rule. In this dualism lies the originality of the British system. This is expressed by the co-existence of schools privately founded and funded, often of religious origin, whose uncontrolled growth ('administrative muddle', according to Adamson) reached its height at the end of the nineteenth century and necessitated reform from above, and alongside them schools open to all as a result of increasing State control and involvement in education. This involved the increasing control of education by the central government and resulted in the creation of the Board (later to be the Ministry) of Education in 1899 and three fundamental documents, the three great Education Acts: Forster's of 1870, establishing a system of primary education for all, Balfour's of 1902 and Butler's of 1944. Thus there were three stages: State assistance (1870–1902), State supervision (1902–44), State control (post–1944). The private sector, far from being swept away by successive reforms, managed to survive, though it had to accept partial integration. All this accounts for the complicated though infinitely adaptable structure of the whole system, as well as its comparative independence.

Another way of looking at the subject is to see the school as the battleground of the great religious controversies which shook the country from the mid-century onwards: Dissenters against the established Church, champions of secular as against religious education, Catholics against Protestants, Latitudinarians against Fundamentalists. Every shade of opinion, every cause was involved in the semi-political, semi-theological battle between Churches, sects, pressure groups, and political parties.

A third way of looking at the educational system is to study it in its relations with society as a whole, and the way it embodies the prevailing values of that society. It is on this aspect that we hope to shed a little light. For systems of education both reinforce the structure of society and mirror its features; but in England, more than elsewhere, they have been, and to some extent remain, a decisive cause of inequality.

The basic fact is that there was not just one single system. There were two, functioning independently side by side, but not communicating at all. One was for the élite, the other for the masses. The first was elaborate, expensive, richly endowed and intended for the children of the ruling class; these it received at a tender age in 'preparatory schools', then led them to that key institution the 'public school' where their character received its crucial stamp, then perhaps it led them to a university, probably one of the two oldest, Oxford or Cambridge. The other system, for ordinary children, was rudimentary, brief and free; it turned on the 'elementary' school and finished when the child went out to work at the end of his thirteenth year. This system included the 'Sunday schools', and some technical and higher primary schools. Thus two educational channels existed side by side quite independently, separated by water-tight barriers – a scholastic segregation that both typified and aggravated social segregation. Disraeli's 'Two Nations' remained, becoming (as education progressed) even more rigidly circumscribed and kept apart by an unbridgeable divide. Finally the very slight democratization induced by the spread of popular education in the last third of the nineteenth century was amply offset by the control exercised by the ruling class over the very structure of teaching. It was fruitless to enlarge the house of education if all the best rooms were to be reserved for the privileged, while the masses were relegated to the outhouses and basements. This was why, apart from a little diversification due to increased demand, education kept the same structure as developed between 1840 and 1870 right up to the end of the century, and in many aspects on until the inter-war period.

The public schools were the centre of élite education. Their popularity and their reputation were enormous. In the classic troika – primary ('preparatory school'), secondary ('public school'), higher education (university) – it was the second that really counted; for the public schools were the moulders of the nation's ruling and managing classes. The university was merely complementary, only necessary for those destined for careers in government and politics, the Church, Law and science. But to achieve or to keep one's place among the élite it was essential to have been at the right sort of school. After that one was accepted into the charmed circle, for one was stamped with an easily recognized mark of social superiority. These key centres in the social edifice have rightly been compared to Catholic seminaries. Future leaders were being prepared there for their life's work, and in this lay the originality of the public schools. They aimed at shaping character as well as brainpower, bodies as well as minds, team spirit as well as individuality. In phrases of memorable pride the Clarendon Commission of 1864 praised the merits of these establishments where specifically English qualities were being inculcated; and the same sort of language was being used fifty years later:

. . . their capacity to govern others and control themselves, their aptitude for combining freedom with order, their public spirit, their vigour and manliness of character, their strong but not slavish respect for public opinion, their love of healthy sports and exercise. These schools have been the chief nurseries of our statesmen; in them, and in schools modelled after them, men of all the various classes that make up English society, destined for every profession and career, have been brought up on a footing of social equality, and have contracted the most enduring friendships, and some of the ruling habits of their lives; and they have had the largest share in moulding the character of an English Gentleman.[15]

The public school system itself had its own pecking order. There were two tiers. At the top were the schools frequented by the upper classes – aristocracy, gentry, and upper middle class – shaping them to be the future heads of the Army, the Church of England, senior politicians and the flower of the professions. The majority of young men destined for such exalted futures went to nine great schools, the oldest and the smartest. This 'sacred nine', reformed by the Clarendon Commission (1861–4) comprised seven boarding schools: Winchester (founded in 1382, with the motto 'Manners Makyth Man'), Eton (1440), Westminster (1560), Charterhouse (1611), Harrow (1571), Rugby (1567), Shrewsbury (1552), and two day-schools, St Paul's (1509) and Merchant Taylors (1561).

Ranking below these was a very large number of other public schools. Usually of recent foundation, they were intended for the sons of the middle classes, from among whom would emerge top and middle-ranking administrators, lawyers and businessmen. There were three categories of such schools: (1) grammar (or endowed) schools, ancient foundations which had been modernized in the nineteenth century; (2) proprietary schools (private but non-profit-making, often owned by a collective body), founded after 1840 for middle-class boys and as a kind of riposte to the ancient aristocratic institutions; and (3) some private schools (belonging to individuals who ran them for profit). Among the better known of these public schools for the young of the middle classes (listed by the Taunton Commission of 1864–7) were Cheltenham (1841), Marlborough (1842), Rossall (1844), Radley (1847), Lancing (1848), Epsom (1853), Clifton (1862), Haileybury (1862) and Malvern (1865). Some were of Nonconformist origin, others specifically Anglican, such as Lancing and Marlborough (the latter specializing in taking sons of clergymen). The Roman Catholic schools, Stonyhurst (Jesuit) and Ampleforth (Benedictine), gained considerable reputations. Old grammar schools, such as Tonbridge and Uppingham, were being reshaped, the latter by a great educationalist, Thring, who was headmaster from 1853 to 1887. Two other great educational innovators, who influenced the whole public school system, were Thomas Arnold of Rugby (whose creed was stated in the words 'what we must look for here is (1) religious and moral principles, (2) gentlemanly conduct, (3) intellectual ability'),[16] and following him Sanderson of Oundle (1892–1922). Thus was built up a corporate sense of similar standards and similar ideals among all public schools. These were accepted as such by the attendance of their headmasters at the Headmasters' Conference, which by 1914 totalled 200 schools.

Notwithstanding differences in organization, social status of pupils and constitutional origins, these schools all produced a rather similar type and had very similar teaching methods. The aim they all shared was to inculcate in the future ruling class a common set of standards that emerged from the union of aristocratic and bourgeois values. Aristocratic influence appears in the 'élitism', the strong feeling of superiority and responsibility towards others, the conviction, carefully nurtured, of being a 'natural ruler', and withal a touch of chivalry and religious feeling. The ideal was the Christian English gentleman (so far as the use of both adjectives was not pleonastic!). Godliness and manliness, these were the two basic virtues to be cultivated, but the bourgeois virtues also played their part. For the young had to be prepared for a world of competition and enterprise, so great importance was attached to anything that encouraged competitiveness and personal rivalry, both in the classroom (examinations, prizes, debating societies) and on the playing field (athletics, school matches, and above all cricket and rowing). Although at Rugby in 1870 17 out of 22 hours of study were devoted to the classics, reflecting an aristocratic view of culture, modern subjects that conformed to more material and bourgeois needs were gradually introduced – mathematics, science and modern languages. The moral atmosphere, deriving from a system of 'prefects', group self-discipline and 'fagging', combined a cult of sturdy independence – self-control, courage, stoicism and the 'stiff upper lip' – with an ethic of sociability and 'fair play'. An evangelical exaltation of sacrifice and self-reliance thus went hand in hand with the boosting of each school's highly individualistic spirit. Since the aim was the formation of strong characters, it was constantly rubbed in that life was a struggle, calling for the pugnacious spirit of a medieval baron combined with the ruthless competitiveness of a modern bourgeois. Such was the lesson imbibed at the feet of Thomas Arnold by Hughes, the author of *Tom Brown's Schooldays*. Published in 1857, it became a bestseller, popularizing the current ideals of Rugby among the young. Such too was the atmosphere that pervaded Kipling's novel, *Stalky and Co.* (1899). Later on, his famous poem *If* was to celebrate manly courage as inculcated (with a certain degree of brutality and conformist pressure) in all the public schools of the kingdom.

In deep contrast to this world of education for rulers, organized teaching for the children of the lower classes was designed to instil obedience and acceptance of their lot, and to produce manual workers. The elementary school syllabus aimed at teaching the rudiments needed for performing the basic tasks of an industrial society. Not that every door to the advancement of freedom through education was closed. The tremendous efforts made after 1870 resulted in the opportunity of a place in school for every child of every class, street arab or respectable working class. They created an education that was gratis and compulsory. Truancy was reduced, though the 'half-time' system, common in northern industrial areas, persisted until its abolition in 1918. Another good result was the reduction of illiteracy, and England's record in this was good. By the end of the first half-century, two-thirds of all adult males could read and sign their names. In 1871 the Registrar-General recorded 80 per cent of males and 73 per cent of females able to read and write. By 1897 the number of illiterates had fallen to a mere 3 per cent.[17]

However the mission assigned to popular education was scarcely affected. From the time the education reform of 1870 – school for all – was set in train, to the beginning of the new century, the goal remained the same: to prepare the future worker by providing him with the necessary, but scanty, educational equipment. Hence the themes set out in 1861 by the Newcastle Commission on primary education, when it referred to 'the peremptory demands of the labour market'[18] or, a year later, by Robert Lowe, one of the pioneers of reform, who proclaimed 'we do not profess to give these children an education that will raise them above their station and business in life . . . but to give them an education that may fit them for that business'.[19] One finds much the same sentiments half a century later among the statements of the teachers' union, which, in the middle of the Edwardian era, stated as a self-evident aspect of primary education: 'Six million children are in the public elementary schools of England and Wales. They are the children of the workers, to be themselves England's workers a few years hence.'[20] The inescapable conclusion is that the whole system was avowedly geared to the perpetuation of the class system and social inequality.

It was the same with the Sunday schools, whose pupils came largely from the working class. In 1851 there were 2.4 million registered pupils, with an actual attendance of 1.8 million; in 1887 three out of four children were registered, a total of 5.2 million, with an attendance rate of two-thirds.[21] In these classes the emphasis was on religious instruction, play and general education, rather than on the three Rs, the need for which was by now fairly well met.

In a more positive sense portents of change were beginning to appear round about 1900: a movement towards local colleges of technical and further education; the undoubted growth of secondary education, which was beginning to be penetrated by the lower middle classes; and the birth of adult education, thanks to a triple alliance between the trade unions, the Co-operative Movement and the University Extension Boards, resulting in 1903 in the creation of the Workers' Educational Association. However these fragile innovations did very little to shake the cultural monopoly of the ruling class.

The idea of making education an instrument for planned social mobility was still in the womb of time. The vision of school as a ladder for surmounting the social strata, or as a series of stepping-stones from one sort of learning to another – all these bold dreams had to wait until the inter-war period for their fulfilment.

Sex and death

Nothing throws more light on the deep roots of a society than its attitude to sex and death. The Victorians, faced with these two great and mysterious forces, Eros and Thanatos, chose unequivocally to hush up sex and glorify death. Repression on one side, celebration on the other: a choice dictated as ever by the contrasting fears of the dark forces of creation and destruction. An attitude, one might point out, exactly the opposite of what prevails in England today where, in common with the rest of the western world, death is hushed up and sex glorified – this, too, a panic choice.

A century ago it was certainly difficult to avoid the omnipresence of death. Young and old were struck down, with a mortality rate twice that of today. Innumerable orphans, men and women stricken in the prime of life, mothers dying in childbirth, children in the cradle, a mass of widows and widowers, all helped to conjure up the vision of the abhorred Angel of Death. But as the poor would say, somebody did well out of it – the undertakers. In Great Britain 150,000 infants died annually before reaching their first birthday. Another significant statistic was the count of widows and widowers. The global proportion in the population (about 6 per cent) scarcely changed, but in less than a hundred years the age distribution altered strikingly. (It should be noted that the figure for those in the age group 15–44 would be considerably higher in 1871 were it not for the large number of second marriages.)

Death was not, however, accepted as just an inevitable feature of the daily scene. It was universally solemnized, indeed glorified, as part of the ritual of community life. Hence the scenes described in literature and popular art, interminable agonies, edifying ceremonies with the entire

Table 4 Distribution of the widowed population by age group, 1871–1966[22]

Age group (widows and widowers)	1871	1931	1951	1966
15–44 years	19	10	5	3
45–64 years	42	40	33	27
over 65 years	39	50	62	70
	100	100	100	100

family, children and servants, all gathered round the death bed; the hours spent in death chamber vigils, in lengthy funeral services and visits to the cemetery. Not to mention the deep and interminable mourning, so that, among the favourite colours of Victorian ladies, mauves, yellows and pastel greens, black unquestionably took pride of place. This was especially to be seen at funerals, which were always solemn and sometimes extravagant: huge baroque hearses, lavishly decked out with fancy harness and enormous draperies, followed by processions of mourners swathed in black crêpe veils. Such ostentatious display was not, we may observe, indulged in only by the wealthy. If the deceased was a person of some standing, the family of course excelled itself in funerary pomp; but even among the working classes, where burials were an occasion for colleagues and neighbours to congregate with the double aim of paying homage to the dead and asserting their own collective vitality, a lot of money was spent on the funeral, often the equivalent of several months' pay. Hence the attraction of Friendly Societies. 'Funeral benefits' were a prior charge, so great was the fear among the poor of being unable to afford a decent funeral. Another sign of the eternal presence of death lay in the great theological battles about the after-life which rolled on throughout the century. Controversy raged about the Day of Judgement. In 1853 F. D. Maurice, the Christian Socialist, was deprived of his professorship in the University of London for expressing doubts about the doctrine of eternal punishment. With God portrayed as a pitiless judge, the fear of eternal damnation was widespread, and the flames of hell haunted the humblest imagination.

Sexuality and death were both involved in a curious custom observed by London prostitutes, showing how some ritual traditions survived, more or less underground, into the industrial era. When one of them died, her fellow streetwalkers organized in her honour a funeral like that of a bride who died before her time. The hearse was decked with white plumes and followed by weeping prostitutes cloaked and veiled in black and adorned with white ribbons. The whole cortège would be protected by an escort of pimps to ward off the missiles and jeers of the respectable women of the neighbourhood.[23] For in Victorian and Edwardian England, where bourgeois morals were widely accepted among the working class, either silence or the double standard applied in matters of sex.

Let us begin with silence. Sex was taboo. It was surrounded with inhibitions and disapproval. It was tempting; it was shameful; it was better to say nothing about it. 'Sensual' meant 'animal'. In *Middlemarch*, George Eliot described how Doctor Lydgate's education had developed in him 'a general sense of secrecy and obscenity in connection with his internal structure'.[24] The body was taboo, and nakedness forbidden. Good form required that one should not talk about such things. One spoke of 'limbs', not 'legs', and rather than 'go to bed', one 'retired to rest'. An incredible degree of prudery and hypocrisy was attained. Triumphant respectability was personified in Mrs Grundy. There was some easing up toward the end of the century, but in social life and on the stage the moral code was strictly enforced. To be proved guilty of adultery in a court of law was enough to break a politician, be he as brilliant as Dilke or Parnell. In 1895 Oscar Wilde served a stiff term of imprisonment for homosexuality. Bernard Shaw's play, *Mrs Warren's Profession* (1893), all the more shocking for denouncing cant, was banned from the stage and remained so until 1925.

These prudish conventions drew additional force from their claim to have a spiritual sanction – the glorification of asceticism and chastity. Ideas about sex had undergone a great transposition. The diversion of Protestant religiosity into a narrow puritan morality caused sex to be treated as a secret and rather shamefaced affair, public reference to which was only justified by the legally sanctified production of children in the family setting. The family became the object of universal panegyric. There were, however, a few exceptions to this rigid code which are worth mentioning. Research into oral tradition shows that morals were rather more free and easy in some working-class circles and among country-folk. Language was more direct, and a more natural and permissive view was taken of relations between the sexes and their biological functions.

The alliance between strictness and hypocrisy bolstered the principle of the 'double standard'. This involved the creation of two separate worlds: in one, chastity and family life; in the other, pleasure and the gratification of the instincts. The first was bound up with the inheritance of property, marriage, and the legitimization of offspring. The second provided an outlet for the sexual impulses. The result was a separate set of morals for each sex. A woman was expected to adhere to a code of rigorous purity; chastity was considered to be a natural attribute, so she had to be sheltered from anything that might impair or defile it. Hence the utter contempt for the girl who had been seduced, and the 'fallen woman'. A man, on the other hand, was perfectly free to combine a happy family life with the pursuit of outside pleasures in the company of women from a different social class. The potency of the 'double standard' consisted in the fact that it not only gave a man unfettered freedom, but also satisfied the basic demands of a patriarchal and bourgeois society, where female chastity was enforced with the utmost strictness, while men were permitted any number of extra-marital affairs, so long as inheritances were not endangered. Moreover the lateness of marriage among the ruling classes provided a further incentive for this sort of behaviour. In short, collective morality, by establishing a clear-cut barrier between marriage and prostitution, established also their absolute interdependence.

This is why the seamy side of Victorian and Edwardian society, for long hidden but now fully exposed, served a profoundly logical purpose, instead of simply ministering to the needs of a few depraved and hypocritical characters. London's thousands of brothels and trysting places earned it the name of the 'whoreshop of the world'. It would have been simple to draw a map of its pleasures. Such a map would have stretched from St John's Wood in the north west where the cosy and discreet villas harboured mistresses and demi-mondaines, not to mention various perversions (especially *'le vice anglais'* of flagellation), then across to the slum haunts of the port of London, after passing through the whole of the West End. There swarms of prostitutes walked the pavements of Piccadilly, Mayfair and Soho, and it was to these that Gladstone, on his way home from the House of Commons, addressed his exhortations to follow the paths of righteousness. There was pornography for sale, well concealed but now known to have been widely diffused, and a white slave trade, the cause of a resounding scandal in 1885. In fact London ran Paris close for the title 'the modern Babylon'.

The 'double standard' was accepted by many without a qualm. 'A French mistress and an English wife, that's the way to live', said an exponent of the theory to Hector Malot.[25] Lecky, a well-known liberal historian, sang the praise of the prostitute with a frankness verging on cynicism: 'Herself the supreme example of vice, she is ultimately the most efficient guardian of virtue. But for her the unchallenged purity of countless happy homes would be polluted . . . .'[26]

However, besides resort to prostitutes (called 'the great social evil'), there were plenty of other ways of enjoying the pleasures of the flesh. One has only to see the number of girls seduced, mostly servants, but working-class and farm girls too. An interesting sign of class differences in sexual behaviour was that illegitimate births were significantly higher in the West End than in the East End. In the working classes the young man usually married the girl he had put in the family way.

Among the aristocracy the libertine tradition was never quite stifled by bourgeois puritanism, but it was now carried on more discreetly. The middle-class ideal, on the other hand, was the 'blushing young maiden'. Woman was transformed into a sexless figure, and there was a lot of truth in the joke about Dickens' heroines – 'angels without legs'. There was also widespread ignorance of the facts of life. Current prejudices distorted even the utterances of scientists: from Dr Acton who, although he was a reputable scientist, remarked, 'Happily for them the majority of women are not much troubled by sexual desire: the best mothers, spouses and housewives know little or nothing of the pleasures of the senses; their strongest feelings are devoted to home life, children and their domestic duties',[27] down to the learned doctor who, just before 1914, told his students at Oxford: 'Speaking as a doctor, I can tell you that nine out of ten women are indifferent to sex or actively dislike it; the tenth, who enjoys it, will always be a harlot.'[28]

If English society chose to exorcize death by surrounding it with the most elaborate ceremonial possible, it did the opposite when it came to appeasing the demons of sexuality; for here repression was the rule. While the mystery of death was aired in endless discussion about survival – the certainty of the life hereafter and of eternal damnation – the mystery of sex was buried in silence. An extraordinary contrast with the England of today. Obscenity has a new meaning: yesterday it was sex, today it's death. Publicity a new object: yesterday death, today sex.

Up till 1914 change came slowly, but, as belief weakened, death became secularized. Cremation was becoming more common, but burial services changed very little. Soon the holocaust of 1914 provided an unexpected chance for funeral pomp at countless ceremonies in which patriotic fervour was combined with a desire to honour the absent dead. The more rapid change in sexual behaviour owed less to new-fangled theories, such as those of Havelock Ellis, the pioneer of sexology, than to social pressures and the struggle for female emancipation.

The end of *Pax Britannica*

Safe in their island world, immune to invasion, the British had enjoyed a peaceful century. True, it was not entirely peaceful, since there had been quite a spate of colonial wars, nicknamed 'Queen Victoria's little wars'. Most of these had been expeditions rather than wars. Only two had been of any seriousness, waged against foes of some size and strength and engaging the attention of the whole nation: the Crimean War and, fifty years later, the Boer War. In spite of heavy casualties (largely due to sickness) most people saw these campaigns as nothing more than routine punishments administered to bring temporarily recalcitrant partners to reason. After 1905 the clouds began to gather in Europe, but the carefree mood continued. Even on the morning after Sarajevo, Monday 29 June 1914, the *Daily Mail* carried the headline, 'The best week-end of the year', and quoted 'the general verdict of holiday-makers' returning from sea-side or country, speaking in euphoric terms of 'the golden sunshine and the elastic quality of the air' on that gorgeous Sunday. Who could dream that the English might soon be involved in a European war?

Ten years had passed since England had begun to lose her comfortable and advantageous position of non-involvement. For a hundred years her European policy had been based on two factors which she had manipu-lated with consummate skill – the strategic position of Britain as an island, and the multipolar system on the Continent. The Foreign Office had devoted all its skill to keeping this situation in equilibrium. Eternal vigil-ance and incessant effort were needed to keep the balance of forces and remain in an independent but commanding position. The idea behind this exercise in geopolitics was that 'the key to success in diplomacy lay in freedom of action, not in a system of formal alliances' (as Henry Kissinger remarks in his book on Metternich[29]). This kind of freedom gave more protection than an alliance, for it left all options open against the day of need. It had given the English a strong sense of security which lasted right up to the outbreak of war, and even after. The web of arrangements woven by Palmerston, Salisbury, Lansdowne and Grey seemed to hold fairly well, and when cracks began to show they were gradually patched up. The *Pax Britannica* had lasted so long, and people were so proud of its many successes over the century that they thought it could last for ever. Admittedly 'splendid isolation' had had to be abandoned at the begin-ning of the century. Faced with the threat offered by dynamic German imperialism to their naval and economic supremacy, England had signed an *entente* with France and had even held staff talks. The Triple Entente with Russia had also been formed. But even though English diplomacy had changed course decisively, and prudently, in moving towards a military alliance in Europe, the nation remained psychologically an island, its gaze fixed on distant seas. There were very few capable of believing that some day soon the country might be dragged into a great Continental war.

In other words the British continued to see themselves as a race apart. They felt no need to boast about this, or give themselves airs about their insular carapace, or behave condescendingly towards other countries. It was simply that for them *Pax Britannica* was upheld by three apparently indestructible forces: the sea, the fleet and the Empire. The first was a force of nature, the other two were forces of their own creation. This was why Germany's new naval ambitions not merely alarmed a people that firmly believed 'there could only be one ruler of the waves,' but shook their whole sense of national security. As Churchill said in a speech in

1912, a fleet was a necessity for Britain, but a luxury for Germany. It was the British Navy, he said, that made Britain a great power, while Germany was already a great power, respected and honoured all over the world, before she had a single ship.[30] Such was the pride and affection in which the Royal Navy was held; and such were the reasons behind the enthusiastic support from all parties – Conservative, Liberal and even Labour – for a massive shipbuilding programme aimed at maintaining Britain's naval supremacy. In July 1914, a few days before the outbreak of war, the crowds were treated to the thrilling spectacle of a 45-mile long line of warships at Spithead, the most formidable concentration of sea-power the world had ever seen.

With its many peoples, its great material resources, its political unity, the Empire stood as the pledge and symbol of a power that stretched across the world. The British were utterly confident in its strength, its permanence, its ability to stand up to any shock – an assurance well expressed in George V's message to his people at the outbreak of war: 'I shall be strengthened in the discharge of the great responsibility which rests upon me by the confident belief that in the time of trial my Empire will be united, calm and resolute and trusting in God.'[31]

But in spite of eloquent statements and bellicose cries of 'Down with Germany!' from excited crowds, there was deep anxiety. It was the end of *Pax Britannica*, the end of *Pax Europaea*. 'The lamps are going out all over Europe; we shall not see them lit again in our lifetime', said Lord Grey on 3 August, and when Britain's ultimatum to Germany expired, the mood changed from *insouciance* to stupefaction. Behind the almost forgotten shadow of war lay a terrifying plunge into the unknown. That afternoon, in a peaceful country village, a farmer's wife drove her pony-cart to the nearest market town to read the latest telegrams pinned up in the post office. She returned in the evening and told her husband the gist of what she had read. After a long silence, her husband, a veteran countryman, a self-made man of independent and pacific opinions, made this prophetic utterance: 'Now nothing will ever be the same again'.[32]

III Through Storms and Crises to Recovery: 1914–55

7 *The search for security and stability*

Twentieth-century blues

> And England over
> Advanced the lofty shade . . .

The shadow that A. E. Housman saw looming up over England was not just the shadow of war, for other clouds were piling up in Albion's sky. The year 1914 saw the beginning of a long and troubled period for English society. For forty years there was one shock after another, and it was not until the early 1950s that the country found a tolerable way of life again, social, economic and international. This is why we have chosen to organize this book in a rather unusual way as regards dates. For these forty years seem to us to have a definite unity. Through wars, depressions and reconstructions we watch the birth of a new society – a society in search of self-improvement, dominated on the one hand by the fight against poverty and on the other by its changed status in the world. At first the troubled islanders try to resist the forces of change; then, slowly adapting to them, they find their efforts faced with further crises. Finally peace is restored (the peace of the 'cold war') and prosperity returns (the dawn of the 'affluent society') with a new and rather precarious harmony established between classes, based on a remodelled distribution of wealth and power. Throughout the period, English society, armed with the traditional values and community feeling that permeated all classes, managed to resist the forces of disruption. These forty years fall between the easy and sheltered pre-1914 period and the mid-1950s, when consensus starts to crumble.

Right up to the First World War, England had enjoyed fortune's favours to an extraordinary degree. Geography and history had combined to shower her with so many blessings that her people had come to see themselves as divinely set apart. Thanks to their island home and their industrial and technological primacy, they had benefited from the incomparable advantages of immunity to invasion, civil harmony, a stable constitution and relatively high personal incomes (in 1900 average incomes were, for the British £43, the French £35, the Germans £30, and the Italians £17[1]). But now the English were reduced to the ranks. The crises of the twentieth century meant the end of their privileged position; and there was worse in store. Under the pressures of war (the 'locomotive of history', as Trotsky called it) movement prevailed over stability. Victorian society, and in many respects Edwardian as well, was founded on a well-defined social order with a fixed division of labour, and with the classes and the sexes knowing their proper roles. This state of affairs, already being called into question by 1900, was roughly shaken by the internal and external blows of war. The period of 'established disorder' began. The good ship Albion ran into rough seas, and fearful efforts were needed from her crew to pilot her through to calmer waters, where there might be at least a partial return to balanced order.

To begin with, the atmosphere had changed considerably in this country which once seemed a model of tolerance and conformity. International discord was reflected in increasing tension at home and in a general scepticism about established institutions. In 1929, after describing several generations of Forsytes, Galsworthy remarked ironically: 'Everything being relative now, there is no longer absolute dependence to be placed on God, Free Trade, Marriage, Consols, Coal, or Caste.'[2] Social and political change was accompanied by bitterness and achieved through brutal and vindictive confrontations. Fear of 'Reds' and 'workers' control' had taken the place of fear of the 'mob'. The political demands of Labour were to split the traditional party system which had provided government by the right and left wings of the middle-class set-up in turn. Two decades were to pass before the almost total elimination of the Liberals restored the old bipartisan game. Liberalism was in full retreat, both as an ideology and as an attitude. It seemed ill-adapted to modern needs which called for organization, regimentation and interventionism. Despite the protests of individualists the State, like a new Leviathan, was gradually interfering more and more in every aspect of life. The public resented this, preferring to trust to instinct and the amateur spirit. Improvisation and 'muddling through' were a national sport raised to the level of a fine art. After 1940 there was a change: planning and rationalization began to infiltrate ministries, local government, big business and industry. Technocracy was looming up. Little by little England adapted herself to the constraints of the modern world. Above all, in the second post-war period, she managed to widen the social basis of power and wealth. The result was a mitigation of social unease and a movement towards a less divisive, more conciliatory society – one that, in its own different way, recalled the harmony and integration of the latter half of the nineteenth century.

In spite of the traumas experienced by Britain in the twentieth century – the trenches, the blitz, the hunger marches, rearmament, the atom bomb, the shedding of the colonies, not to mention the impact of new inventions such as the cinema, the motor-car, psychoanalysis – there remained an internal strength sufficient to withstand the rudest shocks. There was an extraordinary cohesive force in the common fund of values which throughout history has been shared by the whole British community, regardless of political, religious or intellectual differences. When faced with a really serious crisis the English have recourse to their own unique form of defence, that of a national consensus. This was in striking contrast with the other great European nations, none of whom survived this period without domestic upheaval and even bloodshed. Once more England achieved peaceful change steadily without civil disturbance, slowing up from time to time, but never breaking down.

British consensus had three strands: political, national and moral. Politically, in spite of the decline of the Liberal Party, the English remained as attached as ever to individual liberty and parliamentary democracy. In the age of totalitarianism they remained totally unaffected, to the extent that even the strains of ruthless total war were not allowed to diminish the fundamental rights of citizens. With a stubborn confidence in representative government they never ceased to feel the same pride in and respect for the British constitution as did Bagehot and Mr Podsnap in the days of Queen Victoria – in somewhat different language. The same consensus existed at the national level, and under the threat of war there was no need of bellicose slogans to evoke a spontaneous and universal patriotism, combined with a condescending attitude towards foreigners. The nation's history bore witness to this consensus, and every Englishman was imbued with a sense of it; indeed there was almost an official version of it permeating works of scholarship, textbooks and newspapers. More generally, the institutions – schools, Civil Service, local government – perpetuated this feeling of civic community guided by tradition and the common weal. This nourished a powerful attachment to a firmly defined set of rules, observed by all, yet leaving people with a feeling of complete freedom of action. Finally, on the moral plane, the consensus drew strength from ancient Christian and evangelical sources. Even though the Churches' influence had declined the moral message of revivalism remained, either in its Anglican form or in an occasional resurgence of the Nonconformist conscience.

So, one asks, was the England of 1950 so very different from the England of 1920? In other words, did society change fundamentally in those years of instability? One must not be deceived by false appearances. Denis Brogan once said, with penetrating wit, that to 'change anything except the *appearance* of things is the favourite English political method'. This saying can equally well be applied to social change. Deciding what is actually going on – change or immobility, speed or gradualism, disruption or continuity – depends on the viewpoint and, in the end, on the character of the onlooker. At the end of the period a remark in John Osborne's play *Look Back in Anger* throws a vivid light on the foregoing analysis. Alison, the wife of the violently anti-social hero, says to her father, a retired colonel: 'You're hurt because everything's changed. Jimmy's hurt because everything's the same. And neither of you can face it.'

For King and Country: from Flanders' mud to the disillusion of peace

When England declared war on 4 August 1914, it was, to a far greater extent than for the other combatants, a profound break with the past. The liberal way of life, an insular independence, a tradition of peace, all were threatened. The country was unprepared for war, militarily, economically, and psychologically. The British Army consisted of 250,000 men, dispersed all over the world, and the actual expeditionary force sent to France only amounted to 100,000 men. But within a few months the huge machine was functioning and the peace-time industrial economy was mobilized for war. State control replaced *laissez-faire*. In 1916 conscription was imposed. Nine million men were called to the colours (6 million from Great Britain, 3 million from the Empire). It soon became clear how high the stakes were – total victory or annihilation – so that victory could only be won at the cost of a gigantic, almost superhuman effort by the entire nation. Everyone was struck by the apocalyptic nature of the conflict. Some years later, Winston Churchill, in his book *The World Crisis*, recalled its unmitigated violence. The 'Great War', he wrote, had no parallel in history: it differed from all previous wars because of the terrible power of the weapons of destruction employed. The rights of civilians and neutrals were brushed aside. Merchant ships, public buildings, hospitals were shelled or bombed. Poison gas, aerial bombardment, blockade – no weapon was too awful to use. 'In short', he concludes, 'all the horrors of all the ages were brought together.'[3]

It was those actually engaged in the fighting who were the first to whole, in which all social groups should be merged into one. Yet they lost no opportunity to emphasize the gap between lower middle-class respectability and the dreadful stigma of being labelled 'working class'.

The working class

Manual workers gained no advantage from forming a majority of the population, for, as ever in the past, theirs was a world apart, socially isolated and the victim of two basic laws, insecurity and dependence. In it one submitted and toed the line. Here were to be found all those to whom an industrialized society delegated the material tasks of manufacture and distribution. Their world was bounded by the inert matter they handled. They felt segregated from other social categories whom they judged to be above them and 'privileged' ('white-collar' workers and 'gentlemen'). Their outlook was confined by factory discipline to the dull performance of dull repetitive tasks. In this world of unchanging monotony consciousness of class, of belonging to a community that shared identical work and, even more, an identical destiny, was keen and enduring. The depth and fervour of such feelings are well described in D. H. Lawrence's account of the Nottinghamshire coalminers in *Sons and Lovers* (1913), in Llewellyn's Welsh miners in *How Green was my Valley* (1940), and in Richard Hoggart's *The Uses of Literacy* (1957) on West Riding. There were, of course, blatant regional differences. There were, especially between the wars, cases where contrasts between declining and expanding regions were superimposed on contrasts between traditional local peculiarities. As Peter Mathias has justly remarked, one's ideas about England's social situation in this period depended entirely on where the spotlight was turned.[12] There was a wide difference between the shipbuilding yards of Jarrow on the Tyne – 'the town that was murdered', in the vengeful words of its Labour MP, Ellen Wilkinson – and the light industries of Slough on the outskirts of London. Similarly, there was an enormous difference between the standard of living of the workers of Merthyr Tydfil or Greenock and those of Oxford or Coventry. But in spite of these quite wide differences there was a solid community of feeling, a consciousness of rejection and neglect, which persisted unassuaged right up to the 1950s.

During this third of a century, one can distinguish two periods in working-class history. The first, from 1921 to 1940, was dominated by the spectre of unemployment. There was nothing new about unemployment and its hazards, which had been a concomitant of working-class life since the beginnings of industrialism. But now unemployment assumed massive proportions, far greater than anything the world of labour had ever experienced, so that these two decades were of crucial and far-reaching importance. Not only did unemployment seem like some dire plague from which none could escape, the spectacle of millions of people con- demned to the utmost distress being felt as the worst sort of scandal; but in addition this historic experience was to leave lasting marks, even beyond the generation of those who had suffered. The fear of losing their jobs haunted people long after the policy of full employment had been

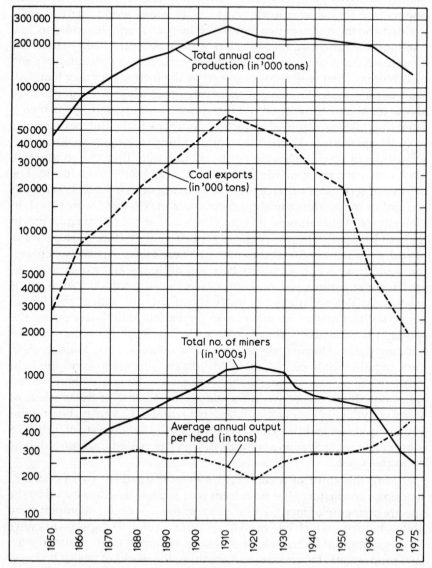

Figure 9. The coal industry in Great Britain, 1850–1974

implemented. Even today many restrictive practices and much trade-union behaviour are due to the recollection of those dark years, deeply engraved on the collective memory.

What gave this particular epidemic of unemployment its intolerable character was that it was as widespread as it was lasting. Whole regions were devastated: the Welsh mining valleys, Lancashire (in Wigan one man in three was 'on the dole'), the steel industry, the shipyards of Tyne and Tees, the Scottish Lowlands (in Glasgow nearly half the population was affected by unemployment). In the coalmines of Bishop Auckland (County Durham), out of 33 pits normally employing 28,000 miners, only 13 were working – and then not continuously – giving employment to 7,000 only. Alongside those lucky ones who were only jobless for a short time, there were two groups who had no hope of escape. On the one hand the young: some had never worked because there was no work for them, others had found unskilled jobs between the ages of 15 and 20, paid at juvenile rates, only to find themselves on the streets when they were adult and had acquired some qualification. On the other hand there were the quasi-permanently unemployed: in 1932 there were 300,000 who had been without work for over a year, and in 1933 there were 500,000. By 1936 there were still 340,000 in that situation, i.e. one man in every four; in that year 53,000 had had no work for more than five years and 205,000 for between two and five years.[13] In all the distressed areas there was a gloomy atmosphere of sadness, of bored resignation and despair. Forced inaction led to demoralization. In the streets of towns, large and small, the unemployed walked aimlessly up and down:

> They lounge at corners of the street
> And greet friends with a shrug of the shoulder
> And they empty pockets out,
> The cynical gestures of the poor . . .
> They sleep long nights and rise at ten
> To watch the hours that drain away.
>
> (Stephen Spender)[14]

Beggars in rags sold matches, boot-polish, boot-laces; pilferers took bits of coal from railway trucks in sidings. In little Welsh towns one saw miners sitting on the pavements endlessly singing songs such as 'Land of our Fathers' to pass the time. Everywhere one found shops closed and houses shut with their windows boarded up. Long queues formed alternately outside labour exchanges and cinemas. The only thriving businesses were pawnbrokers and bookmakers; for in this pointless life of unending idleness and waste people took desperately to betting, in the pathetic hope of the piece of luck that never turns up. Instead of the miracle came demoralization and a feeling of helplessness, witness

Walter Greenwood's *Love on the Dole*, a proletarian novel about life near Manchester, or George Orwell's *The Road to Wigan Pier* about Lancashire and the Sheffield area. Working-class life was not all unemployment, and there were some sheltered and prosperous regions like the South East where workers in expanding industries experienced a sharp rise in their standard of living. All the same the memory of unemployment left its mark on all alike.

This is why the policy of full employment, which started in 1940 and was more fully implemented after the war, represented a fundamental change in working-class life. Henceforward people felt that they would not lose their jobs, or if they did want a change they would find another job. There was also an all-round rise in the standard of living and near-extinction of 'primary poverty', that is poverty due to a lack of the basic necessities of life. The Rowntree social surveys based on research in the city of York showed that the proportion of the working-class population living below the poverty line had fallen from 31.1 per cent in 1936 to 2.8 per cent in 1950. In 1936 unemployment was the cause in 29 per cent of the cases; in 1950 there were none in that category, but two cases of poverty out of three were due to old age.[15]

This transformation of working-class life in the 1940s had three causes: the principal one was full employment, but there were also movements in the level of wages and there was the extension of the social services. The Welfare State gave really effective protection against the major hazards of existence. The real wage of the manual worker increased, but those at the bottom of the ladder, the worst paid, gained proportionately more than the rest. The difference between the pay of the unskilled and the skilled worker, which up till then had been substantial, was markedly reduced. This was partly because the advance of technology, with the development of the mechanized and later automated production line, had introduced intermediate categories of semi-skilled workers so that there was no longer any sharp distinction between those who were highly skilled through apprenticeship or training and those who had no skill at all. It was largely due to pressure from the big unions and public opinion that wide differences in pay disappeared – nominal pay at least, for the skilled worker got round this change by winning bonuses. Women's pay evolved along the same lines as that of men. They were heavily discriminated against, earning about half a man's pay in the years 1930–5. As a general rule the wages of all the lower-paid workers rose more sharply than that of the medium- and higher-paid.

As regards hours of work, 1919 was the key year. There was a major reduction at that date: from the 9-hour day and 54-hour week to the 8-hour day and a week that was sometimes of 46½ hours and sometimes of 48. This was the moment when the steel industry changed from two shifts of 12 hours to three shifts of 8. But it took thirty years to reach the next stage. The working week remained the same until after the Second World War; then it fell to 44½ hours, and round about 1968 to 40½. In contrast improvements in holidays came earlier, in the inter-war period. The granting of holidays with pay became more common, and almost universal after 1945 (a fortnight on average). Leisure activities remained much the same until the invasion of the working man's home by television during the 1950s. The sacred trio – pub, sport and betting – had almost acquired the status of a religion. Occupational hobbies also remained much the same: miners continued to breed whippets and railwaymen cultivated their allotments. Pigeon racing, football matches, trips to Southend or Blackpool were widespread pleasures.

It can be said that there was a twofold process at work after the Second World War. On the one hand, in contrast to the bitter conflicts of the inter-war years, the world of the manual worker was found to be more integrated with the life of the nation, sharing more of its main values. Proletarian poverty seemed to be a thing of the past, since everyone had food and work, a reasonable standard of living, genuine social security and considerate treatment by the powers that be. On the other hand the climate of working-class thought, its culture, language, family life and collective institutions, such as the trade unions, were little changed. As Ferdynand Zweig and Richard Hoggart found, the working class was still deeply imbued with its own exclusive class culture and with the conviction of belonging to a distinct community that was quite apart from the middle-class universe. It was the feeling of having a status rather than an ideology that drew this reply of a timber porter to a sociological inquiry: 'I am not a Socialist, I am Labour.'[16]

Rich and poor: an island of lords or a country of Mr Smiths?

If one is to draw any long-term conclusions about a society as stratified as the English, it is essential to try to find out how class differences have arisen. In other words, what have we to learn from the study of the distribution and amount of wealth in different social groups at different periods? Nobody will deny that the Great Britain of the pre-1914 era, with its glaring social contrasts, well deserved the title of 'a paradise for the rich'. Disraeli's 'Two Nations' lived on, side by side, separated by an almost unbridgeable gulf. However, following two world wars, some democratic pressure and great economic change, there were some signs after 1918 and many more after 1945 of a narrowing of social differences and some cracks in the stratification. The key question of twentieth-century society is this: has there been a reduction of inequality or has it continued, unchanged but skilfully disguised? One can see great

Table 5 Social hierarchy and size of income from the seventeenth to the twentieth century (numbers)[17] 1688–1867: England and Wales 1908–70: the UK

	1688			1803		
Social class	Average income per family (£)	No. of families (in '000s)	Total income received (£ million)	Average income per family (£)	No. of families (in '000s)	Total income received (£ million)
1. Aristocracy	370	17	6	1,220	27	33
2. Middle ranks	60	435	26	195	640	125
Agriculture	52	330	17	119	320	38
Industry and commerce	80	50	4	279	240	67
Professions	91	55	5	250	80	20
3. Lower orders	13	920	12	39	1,350	52
Total	—	1,372	44	—	2,017	210

	1929			1938		
Social class	Personal income (£)	No. of incomes (in '000s)	Total income received (£ million)	Personal income (£)	No. of incomes (in '000s)	Total income received (£ million)
Aristocracy and upper middle class	10,000 +	10	221	10,000 +	8	163
	2,000–10,000	100	378	2000–10,000	97	361
Middle class	1,000–2,000	199	237	1,000–2,000	183	247
	500–1,000	508	312	500–1,000	539	361
Lower middle class	250–500	1,527	404	250–500	1,890	631
Lower middle class, skilled workers	125–250	4,925	980			
Semi-skilled, unskilled, unemployed	125 –	11,600	1,170	250 –	20,300	2,613
Total	—	18,869	3,702	—	23,017	4,376

* Average income per family or household
1,000 + : more than £1,000
500 − : less than £500

the encouragement of rivalry between 'houses'). The teachers in these establishments, since they came mainly from the middle and lower middle classes, were well disposed to this kind of imitation of a model handed down from above. Some such schools, too strenuously 'aping their betters', managed only to caricature them, achieving sort of 'poor men's public schools'.

Furthermore the result of educational practice was to inculcate a middle-class mentality, a middle-class speech and a middle-class ethic. Wasn't conformity with current social attitudes the surest way to success? Consequently a school, even when it had a proportion of working-class children, would act as an integrating force, impressing on the pupils the prevailing values of the middle class. This was so much the case that Labour, which all through the inter-war period had pinned its hopes on the opening of the grammar schools to the children of the working classes (and its own future militants), started to back-pedal on the idea when they found that what it was really doing was to encourage individual ambition and absorption into the middle class. Democratization at that stage was mainly benefiting the lower middle classes.

The secondary educational system, as envisaged by governments and the planners of education between the wars, depended on a method of selection that was supposed to give every child the chance his or her abilities deserved. All depended on the criteria determining the way in which the selection and guidance of the children were carried out. It was widely believed that, thanks to the discoveries of psychology and pedagogy, 'scentific' and hence impartial criteria were available. Experience showed, however, that instead of measuring aptitudes they unwittingly reflected the child's socio-cultural background. There were three stages in this educational development. Between the wars official policy was concentrated on finding out which of the children of the masses were fittest to be offered places in grammar schools, while the rest were to be provided with a post-elementary education. The system thus consisted of two levels – élite and masses – not much different from the Victorian system, except that there was more scope for assisted and scholarship pupils at the secondary level, and hence intelligence tests and various selection methods were designed to reveal latent talent. After 1944 there was a second stage. Every child went to a primary school up to the age of 11; after that each one went to one of three different types of secondary school, according to his or her abilities: academic ('grammar'), modern or technical. It soon became evident that this system had two major shortcomings. On the one hand the three separate types gave rise to a new social hierarchy, for in spite of all the promises of equality of level and status ('parity of esteem') the secondary grammar schools were immediately invested with a superior status, while the 'secondary moderns' suggested second best. This appearance of inequality was given reality not only by the results of selection – middle-class children going to secondary grammar schools, working-class children to secondary moderns – but also by the qualifications of the teachers. Direction to a secondary modern involved the double stigma of social and academic failure. So a new idea came into being in the early 1950s. The basic concept was a single school with pupils of all abilities under one roof, and able to offer every variety of educational choice. This was the 'comprehensive school'. Unification seemed to be the only way to achieve democratization, though it may be remarked that the private education provided by the 'public' schools stayed outside . . . and above. Although some advance had been made, there was still an inherent élitism in the educational scene, not to mention the fact that teaching methods and selection systems continued to favour the new middle-class meritocracy at the expense of the socially deprived.

Higher education expanded proportionally with secondary. In 1900 there were 20,000 university students, in 1938, 50,000, in 1955, 82,000, and by 1962 the total had jumped to 118,000 (see Figure 13).[17] But most of the new students came from the middle and lower middle classes rather than from the working class. Only 25 per cent were sons or daughters of manual workers, though the manual workers formed 75 per cent of the population. This percentage remained unchanged from 1928 to 1960. Once again the children of the masses had benefited less than those of the better-off.

Finally, mention must be made of two educational sectors where democratization and the diffusion of culture were undoubtedly more successful. One was that of adult education. Partly as a result of the strength of working-class organizations and partly, no doubt, in reaction against the avowed élitism of national education, the English pioneered popular education of a cultural kind. The principal organizations were 'extra-mural studies', run by the universities, and the 'Workers' Educational Association', which had about 60,000 students in the 1930s, and some 100,000 in 1948. In general the movement for adult education accelerated during and after the 1939–45 war; so much so that at the beginning of the 1950s there were about 2 million people taking evening courses, technical training and so on.

There was also a tremendous expansion in the production of books. The number of titles published at the beginning of the century was very rapidly doubled: 6,000 in 1901, 12,400 in 1914. In 1937 it reached 17,000 and was doubled again after the war (there were 35,000 titles in 1973).[18] More and more people used the public libraries: in 1949 the number of books lent out in the whole of Great Britain was nearly 300 million.[19] To take one example – at Plymouth the total went from over 365,000 in 1924 to 1.1. million in 1948. The first paperbacks appeared in 1935 when Allen Lane launched 'Penguins', followed two years later by his 'Pelicans', low-priced and aimed at a wide market. In fifteen years 250 million copies were sold.[20] Besides this there was radio (1 million sets in 1925, 9 million in 1935, 12 million in 1950)[21] and the BBC's cultural programmes. The beginning of the 1950s saw a great increase in television: some tens of thousands of sets in 1950, 4 million in 1955, 10 million in 1960, and by 1970 the total was to reach 16 million (see Figure 13).[22] Henceforward school was to be neither the sole nor the most privileged instrument for the diffusion of culture. The age of 'mass media' had begun.

Secular encroachment on religion

As early as the last quarter of the nineteenth century the edifice of religion was beginning to show cracks, and even signs of eventual collapse. After 1914 the position of the Churches took on an even more alarming aspect. Except in the Roman Catholic minority, religious observance seemed to be increasingly confined to women, the elderly and the lower middle class. There was widespread dissatisfaction not only with devotional and ritual practices but also with the beliefs and the moral instruction dispensed by the various sects. For the perspicacious the symptoms were all too clear. The less the Churches counted on having a future the more they dwelt on the past. So it was that indifference was more strongly resisted and the faith more stoutly maintained in the country than in the town, by women more than by men, by the aged more than by the young. Would it be wrong to talk of the decay of Christianity? It would certainly be an exaggeration, in that time-honoured religious sentiments did partly continue to colour people's mental outlook.

However, collective and personal behaviour both became secularized. Gradually human consciousness became adapted to a laicized world, a world that rejected the supernatural, a world 'without enchantment' (Max Weber's expression), where religion merely provided moral and social sanctions and was thus further deprived of meaning, except to those minorities of believers who still hoped to find in Christianity the answer to their questions on salvation and the future life. The change came about quite gently; no strife, no strong anti-clerical feeling. The decline of religious feeling brought about a decline in sectarian bitterness. The process was not a single movement but had many streams. In spite of a small active minority of atheists the militancy of former days that one associates with the names of Holyoake and Bradlaugh, was entirely lacking. Rejection of religion tended to be confined to the fairly frequent reactions against the odious tyranny of hypocrisy and the conventions.

The great 'sea of faith', which once covered the country, had ebbed until nothing was left but little pools in the midst of deserts of indifference or of marshlands where religion survived only in the shape of religiosity. This inexorable retreat of traditional religious practice was characterized by three different phenomena: first, a rapid falling-off of religious observance, helped by a decline of belief in the basic tenets of Christianity; secondly, the reduction of Christian faith to a rather woolly social ethic; thirdly, a wide gulf between the religious institutions – Churches and sects – and the actual aspirations cherished by the great majority of people.

On the first point, thanks to various pieces of research, we now have data which, however approximate, all point in the same direction, namely a massive decline in church attendance. This, it must be admitted, had already been pretty low among the urban masses ever since the Industrial Revolution. Three surveys in York, carried out by Rowntree, all on the same lines, in the years 1901, 1935 and 1948, enable one to measure the change in a typical medium-sized town over half a century.[23]

Table 10 Number of attendances at places of worship in York by adults in 1901, 1935, 1948

Denomination	No. of attendants			Percentage of members of each denomination		
	1901	1935	1948	1901	1935	1948
Anglican	7,453	5,395	3,384	43.7	42.2	33.1
Nonconformist	6,447	3,883	3,514	37.8	30.4	34.4
Roman Catholic	2,360	2,989	3,073	13.8	23.4	30.1
Salvation Army (indoor services)	800	503	249	4.7	4.0	2.4
Total	17,060	12,770	10,220	100	100	100
Total population of York	48,000	72,000	78,000			
Percentage of population	35.5	17.7	13.0			

Figures relate to persons aged 18 and over

It will be seen that in 1948 churchgoers numbered only one-third of those in 1901. This more or less corresponds with the results of research carried out by Geoffrey Gorer in 1955. He concluded that about 16 per cent of the population were regular churchgoers and 45 per cent intermittent ones (i.e. they attended at least one or two services a year). The remainder, of whom half were adults males, never went into a place of worship, except for funerals and weddings.[24] Another inquiry on Sunday observance carried out in 1957 by the *News Chronicle* produced an average of 14 per cent composed of 9 per cent from among Anglicans, 20 per cent from among Nonconformists and Presbyterians (Church of Scotland) and 44 per cent from among Roman Catholics.[25]

Still more disturbing for the faithful was the muddle-headedness that prevailed over questions of belief. Soon after the Second World War *Mass Observation* did some fairly intensive research in a representative part of London. The results, published in 1948 under the appropriate title *Puzzled People*, showed that although two-thirds of the men and four-fifths of the women believed more or less in God (only 5 per cent were atheists – a figure confirmed by other inquiries) only one out of three had been into a church in the preceding six months, one out of five did not believe in eternal life, and one out of four never prayed. Furthermore, of the agnostics one-quarter occasionally prayed to a God of whose existence they were not sure; one out of twelve sometimes went to church; one out of four thought that Christ was 'more than human', and half of them favoured religious education in schools. In contrast, of the regularly or intermittently practising followers of the Church of England one-quarter believed neither in life after death nor in the divinity of Christ. For many people religion simply boiled down to maxims like 'doing as much good as you can', or 'helping one another' and so on – all of which corresponds to the age-old working-class saying, 'You don't have to go to church to be a good Christian'.[26]

Behind these various symptoms of change one feels a certain personalization of religious feeling. Henceforward it became a matter of free individual choice rather than of melting into the ranks of a conformist body. Another sign of the waning of the Churches' influence was the habit of reducing faith to a collection of humanitarian precepts, or a moral exhortation, or some form of rather sentimental 'do-gooding'. A neo-morality, so widely and thinly spread as to be rather pallid, had taken the place of the austere morality of evangelism. 'The value of any religion depends upon the ethical dividend that it pays', said Sir George Newman, a distinguished Quaker physician. It is true that, worlds apart from this commercial terminology, one often found genuine fervour among the small number of true believers. But in most cases religion, both as belief and practice, became stale. This was due to the liberalism that abolished the absolute, and the desire for a comfortable life that blunted the old imperatives. Gone was the traditional ascetic ideal with its sublimation of desire. But the force of puritanism was so strong that desire had not been liberated. The attempt to find a way between humanism and Christian tradition resulted in a hybrid ethic, with a taint of hypocrisy. This explains why controversy erupted where the two traditions clashed, e.g. on divorce and contraception. Curiously enough rather less was heard about temperance being the highway to salvation. The spirit of evangelicalism was dying. All that was left of it, except among the few who had an inner life, was an outward show of moral respectability.

No sweeping revivalist movement came to the rescue of the Churches either in the Church of England, where defection, in spite of some missionary endeavour, had been strongest, or from the Nonconformist bodies which were all in full retreat. The only such movements (all, significantly, from America) such as Moral Rearmament (introduced in the 1920s by Frank Buchman's Oxford Group) Christian Science, the Jehovah's Witnesses, and Billy Graham's giant interdenominational meetings, all met with a very small response.

The result was a twofold separation: first between the religious institutions, which were often relegated to the role of a hollow façade, and people's religious needs; secondly between the various groups of genuine believers (becoming smaller and smaller) and society as a whole, which paid less and less regard to all forms of organized religion. This caused much lamentation, especially among traditionalists. Some of the more discerning of the faithful saw a positive side to this clear distinction between belief and religion. T. S. Eliot expressed the opinion that the Churches would in future draw their supporters solely from the small section of the population who were dissatisfied with the spiritual emptiness of a hand-to-mouth existence. These would guard and keep their faith and their liturgy alive, apart from the multitude. Graham Greene said much the same from a Roman Catholic point of view about 'Post-christianity' in England.

All through this period only the Roman Catholic Church managed to avoid falling back, and even increased its numbers. The total number in Great Britain increased from about 2 million in 1914 to 5 million in 1955. The figures were even more significant over a longer period. In 1850 there were 600 churches and chapels and 840 priests; in 1913 1,800 and 3,800 respectively; in 1940, 2,600 and 5,900; in 1955, 3,000 and 7,000. In spite of persistent cries of 'Papistry', the allure of the Church of Rome was demonstrated by the number of its converts – a steady 12,000 a year from 1920 to 1955, whereas the figure was only 7,500 before 1914.[27] In addition, the resumption of Irish immigration during and after the Second World War, and the fact that many Poles had settled on English soil, swelled the numbers of the Roman Catholic community. With all this there was still a feeling of isolation, and the community retained the outlook of a minority.

One must not, however, exaggerate the extent of English irreligion, for it was tempered in two ways. One was institutional pressure: public life continued under the aegis of a State Church, and, more importantly, this Church was closely interwoven with the whole fabric of national existence. Even if it got harder and harder to describe the content of orthodoxy – if only because of the diversity of currents within the estab-

Pay Act, which came into force in 1975. Nevertheless it was noticeable that in the decade 1965–75 the salaries of women increased less rapidly on average than those of men. In conclusion let us quote one figure which alone denotes the startling difference that remained between the sexes in the matter of pay and jobs. In 1975 the average earnings of women were just a little more than half of those of men.

11 *Decadence or wisdom?*

Sic transit gloria Britanniae . . .

When, in 1963, *Encounter* devoted a special number to England 'face to face with its destiny', it gave it the provocative but significant title 'Suicide of a Nation?'[1] National introspection was then the fashion, and in some quarters the wind of masochism was blowing at gale force. There was a mood of anxious self-questioning. Was John Bull getting like the character in John Osborne's *The Entertainer* whose jokes nobody laughed at and whose opinions nobody wanted to hear? Even those who refused to look back nostalgically at the past were gloomy and worried about the future. The death of Churchill in 1965 seemed an event of symbolic significance. It brought the islanders brutally up against the fact that a page of their national and imperial history had been turned over, whose glory could never return. While the enormous cortège wound its way through London to the tolling of the bells of St. Paul's, the whole country mournfully reflected that it had lost a part of itself for ever.

Since the calamitous setback of Suez in 1956 the British had been troubled with a painful sense of lost identity. They had experienced a series of disappointments after the hollow euphoria of victory in 1945. The vision of the 'new Elizabethan age' that everyone had hoped for at the Queen's coronation had vanished, and cries of 'decadence' were heard instead. People recalled the words of Matthew Arnold, who at the very apogee of the Victorian era was haunted by the idea of a Great Britain reduced to the role of 'a sort of greater Holland'. Sir Geoffrey Crowther said publicly that England in the twenty-first century would be like Spain in the eighteenth. It was about this time that the Germans invented the contemptuous phrase *'die englische Krankheit'*. That 'the sick man of Europe', the phrase once used to describe the Ottoman Empire, Britain's former client and protégé, should be applied to Britain herself was the very depth of humiliation.

The British were demoralized, not just because of their country's nuclear inferiority at a time when nuclear power meant world power, nor because of the growing evidence of economic weakness, but mainly because they felt that what had been destroyed could never be replaced. They had liquidated their past without planning or even defining their future.

One can discern three reasons for this disenchantment. Loss of the Empire naturally came first, and it was more than just sadness. For a country whose greatness and prosperity had been so dependent on imperial expansion, it was hard to get used to being confined within 90,000 square miles. Even though decolonization had not involved such drama and near-revolution as it had in France, how could the man in the street not be struck by the contrast with the glorious time when, as Ian MacLeod put it, 'at school a third or a quarter of the map was coloured red, and you did get some sort of consolation for being in this bright little, tight little island, and all the old jingo phrases, because of the very vastness of the empire, of which Britain was not only the head but the owner'.[2]

Another reason was that the idea of insularity, isolationism, the 'chosen nation, not like others' gradually lost all credibility. Over the years the British had been deceiving themselves with self-satisfied slogans like 'our world leadership', 'our special position', all aimed at perpetuating the idea that England was a country set apart. They boasted of their privileged position *vis-à-vis* the Commonwealth, and the 'special relationship' with the United States. Even before the Second World War André Siegfried had been amazed at the docility with which the British gave in to all American demands, to the extent that they 'seemed to have decided always to give in'.[3] After the war this dependence was accentuated, the faithful British ally moving more or less openly to the position of a US satellite. Round about 1960, however, the illusion of partnership faded, and all attempts at artificial respiration only led to pointlessly servile behaviour. So England now shared the common lot, and what a shock it was for her to discover that she was just like everyone else! Suddenly she found that she no longer knew her position in the world pecking-order. Old certainties had turned into uncertainties that were all the more painful because 'la nature, la structure, la conjoncture qui sont propres à la Grande-Bretagne' (the character, the structure and the situation of Great Britain), to use de Gaulle's words,[4] made it very uncomfortable for her both to define her new vocation and to discover the joys of being like everyone else. As the years went by, Dean Acheson's cruel epigram about the country 'that had lost an empire and not yet found a role' became more and more pertinent. So it was that, as her myths faded, England learnt resignation. This did not stop her from looking west; for between Europe and America the heart did not always follow the path dictated by reason. C. Le Saché put it well: 'if British xenophobia sets up a barrier the length of the Channel, there is no such barrier on the side of the Atlantic Ocean.'[5]

Yet reason had to prevail. Every analysis, every calculation went to show that England's future lay with Europe. Hence the third cause of dismay – how to manage the difficult re-orientation towards the European community. Apart from a few small groups long convinced of the idea, the move encountered great resistance. This was exacerbated by the tedious sequence of snubs and humiliations imposed by the abrasive character of French diplomacy. However feelings had to bow to facts; and the year 1962 saw a decisive turning-point in the history of Britain's overseas trade. For the first time her exports to Western Europe exceeded those to the sterling area, which roughly meant the Commonwealth. The proportions were: in 1950, 26 per cent and 50 per cent; in 1958, 27 per cent and 37 per cent; in 1970, 41 per cent and 21 per cent; and in 1974, 50 per cent and 18 per cent. The English gradually realized that they were condemned to become Europeans. Thereafter steady progress was made in negotiating the concessions Britain needed before joining the Common Market, leading to the Heath-Pompidou agreement of 1971 and the official entry on 1 January 1973. Finally in June 1975 came the referendum that massively confirmed Britain's entry into Europe.

The threat of stagnation and disruption

One of the arguments in favour of joining Europe concerned the threatening clouds that gathered on Britain's economic horizon. Many saw the Common Market as a sort of life-saving raft. They saw it as an unexpected means of stimulating the flagging economy, which had been going downhill ever since the 1950s. 'Stop-go', 'stagflation', the instability of the currency (closely dependent on the dollar – the pound had been twice devalued, officially in 1967 and *de facto* in 1974), a disastrous balance of payments due to the deficit on foreign trade, and the export of capital giving rise to an increasing external debt – all these adverse trends gave rise to alarm and despondency. There were endless warnings. Among the various Cassandras prophesying doom, Arnold Toynbee raised his voice in denunciation of the typical English vice of always letting things slide until the last minute. All this failed to stir public opinion unduly, unless one bears in mind Arthur Murphy's remark dating from the eighteenth century, when he said with caustic Irish wit: 'People in England are never so happy as when you tell them they are ruined.'

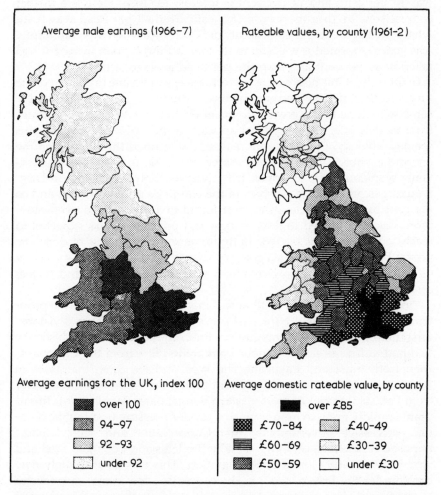

Map 11. The geographical distribution of wealth: differences in the standard of living, by region

Whatever criteria were used to compare national economies, Britain came out badly. From 1950 to 1970 her rate of growth was only three-fifths that of the average of other industrialized countries.[6] The same with her rate of productivity. The second decade (post-1960) was worse than the previous ten years. For example, in 1960–74 the productivity of the United

Kingdom increased by only 30 per cent, in comparision with 90 per cent for Germany and 100 per cent for France. In 1961 the Gross National Product was 26 per cent of the total of what were to be the 'Nine'; by the time Britain had joined them in 1973 it had fallen to 19 per cent; in 1975 it was 16 per cent; and 14 per cent is forecast for 1980. Here is a further comparison. In 1950 the Gross Domestic Product per head was twice what it was in the future community of Six; in 1958 when this community was actually formed it was still more than a third higher; in 1974 it had fallen to 27 per cent less than the per head average of the Six.

In the light of this depressing performance, should one to despair of the future of Britain, now become the 'black sheep' of Europe? There were some who hoped for a great national effort that would drag the country from its lethargy; but in spite of appeals to the 'spirit of Dunkirk' this seemed unlikely. Others, more realistically, pinned their hopes on the enormous energy resources discovered in the North Sea. That was certainly a splendid gift to Britain from Nature. Only discovered in 1965, natural gas provided 57 per cent of the country's needs by 1970, and 90 per cent by 1975. Oil deposits, first found in 1970, seemed even more promising. Oil started to flow in 1975 and production was expected to reach 120 million tons by 1980, a figure definitely in excess of domestic needs. But was this bonanza going to shake the 'stagnant society' out of its obsolescence and into dynamic life? One was, alas, bound to feel certain doubts about this.

On another front, calm until now – that of national unity – two problems had arisen to disturb internal peace and threaten serious divisions. First there was coloured immigration. From 1953 onwards British society had had to face an influx of poor immigrants, first from the Caribbean, then from India and Pakistan. The West Indians came mainly from Jamaica, the Indians were 80 per cent Sikhs, the Pakistanis came either from Pakistan proper or from Eastern Bengal (later Bangladesh). Immigrants rapidly grew so numerous that, under pressure from public opinion, successive governments, first Conservative and then Labour, imposed restrictions on entry. Finally the legislation of 1962, 1968 and 1971 put very strict limits on immigration. This was an absolutely new problem for the British, who, in the course of a few years, saw several towns turning into multiracial communities. Up to the war the coloured population had been negligible – 100,000 in 1931 – but by 1961 it was over 400,000 and by 1971 1.5 million, or 2.5 per cent of the total population of Great Britain. As British subjects they were certainly entitled to all civil and political rights. Moreover, since the Race Relations Acts of 1965 and especially of 1968, all discrimination in matters of employment, housing, services and education was forbidden by law. But the vast flux of coloured people, the differences in standards of living and culture, problems of

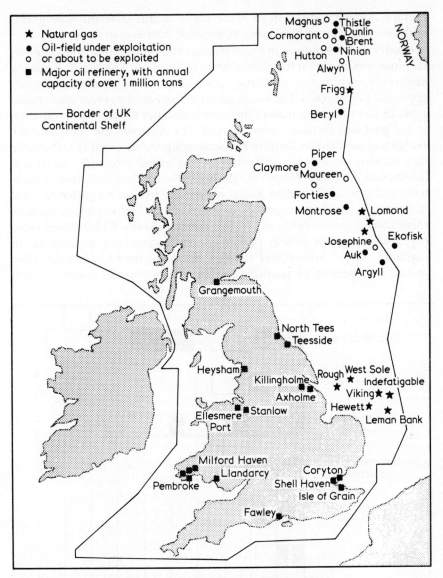

Map 12. Discovery of North Sea oil and natural gas, 1965–75

health, work and family life caused much friction between newcomers and locals, and even outbreaks of racism. The problem was aggravated by the unequal geographical distribution of immigrants, who were mainly concentrated in the six great conurbations, and especially in London and Birmingham. It should be remarked, however, that under the three-fold influence of local authorities, voluntary organizations and public opinion, praiseworthy efforts were made to integrate the immigrants and their families as humanely as possible into British society.

Hardly had the danger of racial tension started to recede than another far more serious threat to national unity loomed up. This was the sudden and noisy resurgence of Celtic nationalism. This phenomenon first appeared in the 1960s, but assumed an unexpectedly graver aspect after 1970. In fact Caledonian and Cambrian resistance to English domination in the past had certainly never ceased. For centuries the Scots and the Welsh had kept alive a flame of national independence, while at the same time making an irreplaceable contribution to the economic, social and intellectual life of the Kingdom. Without these immigrants from mountains and moorlands Britain would never have had such a glittering band of inventors, scholars, engineers, captains of industry, explorers, settlers, missionaries, poets, soldiers. . . . But the races of the 'Celtic fringe' were prepared to accept British parliamentary government so long as, in exchange for the human and strategic resources they had to offer, they gained the benefit of participating in the promotion prospects and

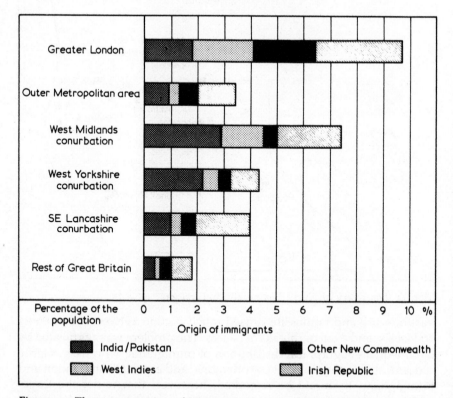

Figure 14. The concentration of immigrants in conurbations, 1971[7]

economic power of a vigorous nation with a vast empire overseas. But after the 1950s the situation had changed fundamentally. Already conscious of being poor relations, ill-favoured by geography, they had been sharply affected by English economic decline, since stagnation worsened the neglect which they already felt was their lot. With all this went feelings of cultural frustration, so that the nationalist movements began to snowball rapidly, particularly among the younger generation. They gained some success at the polls. The first Welsh Nationalist reached the House of Commons in 1966 and the first Scottish Nationalist in 1967. In the parliamentary elections of 1974 the hopes of both parties were encouraged by many more candidates being elected. Neither Welsh nor Scottish separatism seemed in a position to go to the limits of their programme, but they looked as if they might turn the United Kingdom into the Disunited Kingdom.

Class, State and power

During the euphoric expansionist days of the 1950s, a chorus of authoritative voices proclaimed that the days of traditional class and ideological conflicts were over. The country had entered its 'post-capitalist' phase, a dynamic, 'fluid' period heralding the arrival of an 'open' mobile society, ruled by consensus and offering equality of opportunity, where the living standards were middle-range without necessarily being middle class. At the same time, it was claimed, the growing homogeneity of society (itself a result of mass consumption), the unifying power of the techno-structure and the mass media would eventually cut down social distinctions through the standardization of behaviour and leisure activities, and through the universal sharing of common cultural values. The nation was treading the path of social peace – essential, according to Galbraith, if it sought economic growth. This integration process went together with a passive acceptance of the economic system and 'cultural democratization' resulting from mass schooling and mass leisure activities.

This short-term view, contradicted at the very moment that it was formulated, did not stand up to experience, and by the beginning of the 1960s there was a return to earth. Later developments were to show that it was simple-minded to think that growth would lead to an upheaval of the class structure and that affluence would bring general contentment. The truth was that boundaries between social groups had become hazier and less easy to define. These differences, confused by much overlapping, had none of the sharpness and simplicity of Victorian times (though these were relative, as we have seen). Gone was the dichotomy between a working class haunted by pauperism because it lived in a subsistence economy (and often below the subsistence level) and a higher class, bourgeois and aristocratic, with a monopoly of wealth, well-being and leisure. However, to take one example, two excellent social surveys on Banbury (conducted by Margaret Stacey at nearly twenty years' interval, in 1948–51 and 1966–68, and published in 1960 and 1975) show very clearly that in this small but expanding Midland town the differences not only of income and power but particularly of socio-cultural interconnections survived, intact, the arrival of successive layers of population. The research results show very clearly the heterogeneity of two different worlds, each with its own network of social and institutional relationships. On one side there was the middle-class with its Conservative organizations, Anglican churchgoers, Rotarians and Arts Council members; on the other side the world of the masses – Labour bodies, the Trades & Labour Club, the WEA and the Friends of Banbury Hospitals.[8] To take another small example, Arthur Marwick has pointed out that, in the buffets of the House of Commons, one still sees Labour Members taking their cups of tea while the Conservatives treat themselves to gin-and-tonics.[9]

So the whole of the class set-up, sophisticated to the last degree, went cheerfully on its way, just as elaborately stratified as ever. Since the war it had brought itself up to date and adapted itself to the needs of a technological output-minded world. But underneath there always remained the age-old confederacy of birth, money and power. In other words the psychological factor – status and prestige – continued to be allied with the economic – property, income and standard of living. As the crowning triumph of the aristocratic principle, the distinction conferred by name and family was still very much alive. A century before, Disraeli had remarked correctly that England was governed, not by an aristocracy but by the aristocratic principle. This was deeply embedded in the national consciousness and perpetuated itself in a powerful group of forces, institutions and customs, labelled monarchy, House of Lords, honours lists, titles and so on. The strength of the system lay in its capacity for endless extension. From the top to the bottom of the ladder there was a lively consciousness of status. The characteristic that was peculiar to England was that the criterion for discrimination was not related simply to money, as in the United States, but to birth, breeding, occupation, way of life and education. Class was symbolized by a way of being, behaviour, gestures and, above all, accent. People had only to open their mouths to be identified as 'them' or 'us': social origin was betrayed by the first word uttered. In no other country did language, pronunciation and intonation play such a role. A model of social acceptability and good manners was constructed round the 'Oxford' accent, backed up by the BBC accent. The entire educational system, by conforming to the model, added its support.

However, alongside these subjective criteria for determining class affiliations, there were objective inequalities – inequalities of wealth and income, of security and culture. They came under fire, but they continued to flourish in spite of the successes of the Welfare State in reducing extremes of wealth and poverty. As John Westergaard has written: 'Despite a good deal of individual movement up and down the socio-economic scale, most of it short-distance and more of it than before channelled through educational institutions, the substantial inequalities of opportunity arising from social origin have hardly changed over a number of decades.'[10] In these circumstances one feels that for such a society 'opaque' would be more descriptive than 'open'.

At the heart of this society there were two categories deserving closer attention, for it was the interplay of their respective strengths that determined the shifts in real power. On top was the controlling upper class, and more particularly the body of technocrats; and below were the manual workers supported by their unions. Each was backed (though in far from equal strength) by a whole network of institutions and pressure groups, and a precarious equilibrium resulted from the ensuing trials of strength. In short, the power of the State and the techno-structure was faced by its classic opponent – labour.

There were also internal changes in the ruling class. Its influence derived less from its traditional power bases – property, inherited wealth, ability to lead a life of leisure, and conspicuous consumption – than from knowledge, contacts and power of decision. These were the key qualities needed for the management, on a global scale, of giant organizations, as well as for the enjoyment of the advantages and pleasures that went with money and power. A new sort of man was on the increase – the meritocrat. This brought a shake-up in the ranks of the 'charmed circle', and a debate of some importance. Two concepts of the élite were competing, and one was gaining on the other. On the one side, the old aristocratic ideal held good, the ideal of the amateur, born with a gift for leadership, the 'effortless superiority' of the Oxford man. On the other side, the modern ideal was in the ascendant: the competent professional, hard-working and efficient, whose worth was underwritten by merit and good paper qualifications gained in hard competition. In a prophetic book, *The Rise of the Meritocracy*, which caused some sensation when it was published in 1958, Michael Young forecast an awe-inspiring future when, in the name of pure efficiency and by a ruthless system of selection, only the ablest would rise to the top. Was this to be the end of the regime of amateurs, the sudden death of snobbery in its peculiarly English form – which has been called the *Pox Britannica*? Was this to be the triumph of the diploma and the degree? Certainly the change of attitude due to the requirements of technical management, the growth of universities and the multiplication of graduates (the annual number doubled between 1960 and 1970) pointed to a happy future for the meritocrats. All the same, even the new merit-based élite was shaped by the self-same schools and universities that bore, either by tradition or by imitation, the irradicable stamp of upper-class origin. It would appear from recent research, such as that carried out by the Nuffield Foundation on the family and school background of top members of the Civil Service, that even there, where meritocrats abounded, there was still a marked weakness for the semi-aristocratic charms of the public schools and Oxbridge.[11]

The working class found itself up against the twin power of State and Capital, consisting of a huge array of corporate institutions, banks, insurance companies, investment trusts and giant industrial complexes, not to mention the little world of personal connections and interlocking directorships. But even more it found itself up against the privileged holders of knowledge, who had the key to the control of society's future and who had introduced a new version of the division of labour – 'the eggheads and the serfs' in the words of Sir John Newsom.[12] Faced with this alliance of the City and the Treasury, the workers turned to their traditional weapon – trade-union power, in the form of wage claims and by exerting pressure. This was particularly true of the new labour aristocracy, which drew its power both from the technological growth sectors and its key professional positions in the labour hierarchy.

However, for a clear understanding of the deep-seated feelings behind working-class strategy, one needs to shed two widely believed fallacies: one concerns 'embourgeoisement', the other 'integration'. On the first, the work of J. Goldthorpe and D. Lockwood has disposed of a belief that was too hastily deduced from undeniable improvement in standards of living and even what might be called working-class prosperity. One can say unequivocally that there was no 'embourgeoisement' of manual workers any more than there was 'proletarianization' of white-collar workers. As for 'integration', it has been alleged that the philosophy of mass consumption and the brainwashing action of the mass media led to a sameness of outlook. This in its turn engendered an illusion of participation that was really dependence and stifled any creative challenge. In actual fact the working class remained firmly apart, socially, culturally and even materially. The contrast of 'them' and 'us' was still strongly felt. In any case, as Frank Parkin has shown, participation in the dominant system of values was far from preventing the continuation of individual minor cultures. This plurality of sub-cultures was related to particular social or occupational milieux, regional traditions, ideologies, etc. This separateness was further emphasized by two new features: diminishing work satisfaction among a majority of manual workers, and an increasingly home-centred existence. Even so, in the heart of this partially fragmented

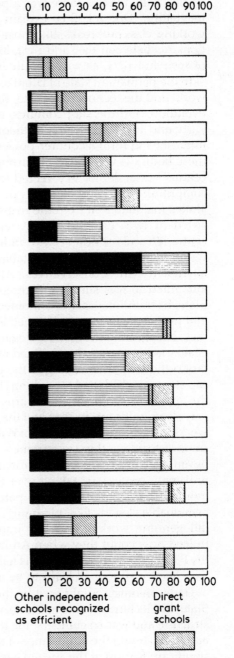

Percentage (taken of the total for whom details are known)

0 10 20 30 40 50 60 70 80 90 100

14 year olds (1967) (England and Wales)

17 year olds (1967) (England and Wales)

School leavers (England and Wales) going to all universities (1965–66)

School leavers (England and Wales) going to Oxford and Cambridge (1965–66)

Vice Chancellors, Heads of colleges and Professors of all English and Welsh universities (1967)

Heads of colleges and Professors of Oxford and Cambridge (1967)

Labour cabinet (1967)

Conservative cabinet (1963)

MPs Labour (1966)

MPs Conservative (1966)

Admirals, Generals and Air Chief Marshals (1967)

Physicians and Surgeons at London teaching hospitals and on the General Medical Council (1967)

Directors of prominent firms (1967)

Church of England Bishops (1967)

Judges and QCs (1967)

Fellows of the Royal Society elected between 1962 and 1966

Governor and Directors of the Bank of England (1967)

0 10 20 30 40 50 60 70 80 90 100

Charterhouse, Eton, Harrow, Marlborough, Rugby, Winchester

Other public schools

Other independent schools recognized as efficient

Direct grant schools

Figure 15. Educational background of leading citizens[12]

world of the masses there was a permanent feeling of exploitation and inequality. Doesn't this explain the ordered violence of periodic working-class outbreaks, like those in protest against the Industrial Relations Act between 1969 and 1974, like the two memorable miners' strikes of 1972 and 1974, as well as numerous smaller eruptions?

In the permanent state of latent or declared warfare between the labour world and the technocratic State, the workers had to take account of the evolution, and the shortcomings, of the two organizations, the Labour Party and the TUC, which in theory were supposed to look after their interests and form a counter-power. The course followed by the first of these bodies is very clear: all through the third quarter of the twentieth century social democracy veered towards a more or less self-confessed compromise with the oligarchs of the productivist system. One could almost maintain that from the 1950s onwards the two-party system consisted of two 'Establishments' regularly alternating in power – one centre-left and the other centre-right – both of them being, in reality, just two branches of the same Establishment, as formerly when Liberals alternated with Conservatives. All that Labour policy under Wilson amounted to was simply enlightened management of the technocratic State. Its traditional tactics combined socialist rhetoric with ultra-cautious and pragmatic measures; it aimed at getting the support of the meritocracy, substituting the modest slogan 'equality of opportunity' for the old egalitarian war-cries. It combined mixed economy with pure parliamentary orthodoxy. It encouraged the progressive elimination of the cloth-cap element which had for so long characterized the Party: henceforward the appeal was to brains, not horny hands. The development at the top was also significant. In 1945 half the Ministers in Attlee's Cabinet were of working-class origin; a quarter in Wilson's 1964 Cabinet; and in 1969, after some reshuffling, there were none – a fine posthumous tribute to Aneurin Bevan, who once expressed horror at the idea of 'lawyers, economists and university professors' taking over the leadership of the Party![13] So the more official Labour sank into patent opportunism, barely masked by fashionable slogans like 'planning', 'social justice', 'expansion', the less did genuine working-class aspirations find an echo in Party policy. Indeed how could they when Anthony Crossland, the most brilliant of the Party's theoreticians, told his fellow-citizens that, as a primary objective, 'we must now all learn to be middle-class'?

Trade unionism might well be the workers' main bastion against the State, but its bureaucratic machinery was itself an element in the techno-structure and was so cumbersome that it lead to apathy among its members. Nor should the importance of this apathy be minimized, for it was a significant feature of the current social situation. At various levels members' participation in decision-making was minimal, most of them doing no more than taking their card and paying their dues. It has been reckoned that, just as in earlier times many workers voted Tory, so after 1945 about 30 per cent of manual workers regularly voted Conservative, and 20–5 per cent of actual trade-union members either Conservative or Liberal. In spite of all this, and however stiff in the joints the unions might be, their claims backed by action made them, in the actual state of society, the principal counter-power. This power was exerted, it is true, in a variable manner, at once progressive and conservative. Their stick-in-the-mud approach was epitomized by their old-fashioned, not to say obtuse habit of aiming at quantitative objectives, often limited to small groups, almost always simply seeking pay increases. At the same time, thanks to a well-tried strike technique capable of causing the maximum disruption of industrial production with the minimum inconvenience to the workforce, the working class was able to give full vent to their sense of alienation and injustice. This is what enabled the workers to keep the Establishment in check, because the latter was warned that it could not misuse its power without suffering for it, and that therefore it would be better to come to terms with the world of labour.

However, alongside this classic instrument of worker power, sturdy but slow-thinking as it was, there arose in the years 1965–75 other forces hoping to form a genuine counterpoise to the weight of the ruling oligarchy. These sniping operations, conducted by determined, inventive and forward-looking minorities, usually operated from the flanks rather than from the front, and their attacks were directed at key-points. The activists tended to be a mixed collection – workers who wanted to see some direct action for a change, young people and women in revolt, intellectuals, technicians on the loose. . . . This sort of action (all part of the 'wind of revolt' mentioned earlier) ran the risk of being defused by the Establishment (to which many of the activists belonged) or by the commercialism of the mass media. However the forces thus set in motion sometimes managed to plant pinpricks in the body of the technocratic State, and so hold the power of neo-capitalism partially in check, but without ever succeeding in shaking the passive conformism of the herd.

An art of living?

'We must cultivate our garden.' No one nowadays seems to have paid more heed to Candide's advice than the English. In renouncing growth at all costs, rejecting the productivity rat race, and in choosing to work less and live more, have the islanders stolen a march on the rest of the world and found a way of wisdom, a quiet shady lane, away from the hellish din of by-passes and motorways? In many ways the present state of England – a calm, well-to-do, relaxed community – seems to bear out John Stuart

Mill's prediction that the slowing-down of growth at the advanced stage of industrial society would lead inevitably to stabilization: within the framework of the 'Stationary State' everyone would accept their place in the economic order because they would rather devote their time to more attractive activities such as culture and the arts.[14] Indeed one only has to re-read Keynes to find that he was the first to proclaim that life was more important than the economy: 'The day is not far off when the economic problem will take the back seat where it belongs, and the arena of the heart and the head will be occupied or reoccupied by our real problems – the problems of life and of human relations, of creation and behaviour and religion.'[15]

There has undoubtedly been a revulsion from purely economic criteria, from an infatuation with technology, from the motivation of pure gain. A passionate acquisitiveness has been replaced by a retreat into one's own garden, or by pursuits of an aesthetic and cultural nature, but everywhere there is a feeling for the importance of calmness, well-being and good sense. In other words, from having been the paragons of industrialization and urbanization in the nineteenth century, the English seem to be moving towards a different model, a cosy genial society, quite unlike the tough conquering race of earlier days. Increasingly the accent is on happiness, but not any sort of happiness. The chosen kind is what one might call the English brand of happiness – leisurely, relaxed, sheltered, not overstrenuous – an existence enjoying equal measures of security and freedom. It is certainly not easy to measure this happiness, nor to discover how far the English think they are blessed with it. But the satisfaction with the way of life they proclaim to the world is plain to see. Witness an inquiry published by the Social Science Research Council in 1974 which put them at the top of the European league for satisfaction with their lot: 85 per cent said they were 'satisfied'; one-third of these were 'very satisfied'.

One can even go further. In showing so much enthusiasm for their 'quality of life', the English have found a new source of national pride; and, curiously enough, there are signs of a resurgence of the old superiority complex. Deeming that they have travelled further along this road than other nations, the islanders are eager to find there new causes for hope. In this way they see themselves fulfilling the proud boast of John Milton: 'Let not England forget her precedence of teaching nations how to live.'[16] In fact in this revival of cultural and spiritual values, in this rediscovery of beauty, simplicity and the importance of human relations, the idea is not simply to drive out Mammon by refusing to become the slave of the money machine and the cash nexus. It functions at a deeper level, as the affirmation of a new ideal, benefiting the community as well as the individual. It is what The Times, in a series of articles devoted to the future of England in 1971, expressed in these terms: in this 'post-imperial' age one can define a new objective,

> the ideal of a country which has raised the real standard of life, rather than the statistical standard of life, higher than any other country. The values which should come first are the human and aesthetic values. Some nations make civilization a by-product of the creation of wealth; Britain is more likely to make wealth a by-product of the creation of a worthwhile civilization. [17]

So, little by little, the mist of failure clears and a modicum of optimism shines through. It is the point made by John Boorman in his film *Leo the Last*: when, at the end, the hero, a prince who has taken up the defence of the oppressed, meets with one failure after another, one of the characters makes the splendid remark that although he has not changed the world, he has changed his neighbourhood!

So the new England of the 1970s is, in many ways, turning its back on its past. Is this the end of Prometheus, and the rebirth of Orpheus? Certainly the new art of living that is emerging has a markedly aesthetic content. Culture and beauty have become major preoccupations of the new generation. The striking burst of creativity that the country has seen since the 1950s in the theatre, in the cinema, in music, classical and popular, art and fashion bears witness to a freedom of expression and a new spontaneity, which show a determination to venture outside well-trodden paths.

In addition, the English are more proud than ever of the tolerance and freedom that are found in their midst, for these qualities form an essential part of the background of their existence. To quote one symbolic fact, the 1887 edition of Baedeker, under the heading 'Passports', says: 'These documents are not necessary in England, except for the purpose of retrieving a letter from a *poste restante*.' Today the identity card is still unknown in Britain. A pluralist society resisting the abuse of power, always ready to fight against any encroachment on the rights of the individual, this is a basic asset of the English art of living. In short, a world that is at once polite and even polished, whose ambition it is to be 'civilized'. Finally, even though England is far from being a paradise, it is undoubtedly a place where it is good to live.

Economy and Society	Culture and Religion	Year
	Butler Education Act	1944
Atomic bomb Family Allowances Act	*Brief Encounter*, a film directed by David Lean	1945
National Insurance Act Creation of new towns	Creation of the Arts Council	1946
		1947
National Health Service End of the Poor Law	Formation of the World Council of Churches	1948
Devaluation of the pound	George Orwell: *1984*	1949
		1950
Festival of Britain	Introduction of the General Certificate of Education (GEC)	1951
Last tram in London The *Comet*: first passenger jet		1952
Ascent of Everest		1953
End of rationing introduced in 1940	Kingsley Amis: *Lucky Jim*	1954
	Start of commercial television	1955
First nuclear power station at Calder Hall	John Osborne: *Look Back in Anger* Alan Sillitoe: *Saturday Night and Sunday Morning*	1956
Consumers Association		1957
	J. K. Galbraith: *The Affluent Society*	1958
		1959
Opening of the M1, the first motorway	Harold Pinter: *The Caretaker* The 'new universities' (1960–5)	1960
		1961
Commonwealth Immigrants Act	Coventry Cathedral (Spence, Piper, Sutherland, Epstein) Benjamin Britten: *Requiem*	1962

Year	Political Life	International Relations and Empire
1963	Death of Gaitskell, Harold Wilson leader of the Labour Party	French veto British entry to Common Market
1964	Elections: Harold Wilson Prime Minister	
1965	Death of Churchill	Unilateral Declaration of Independence in Rhodesia
1966	Elections keep Labour in power	
1967		Decision to withdraw British troops East of Suez (1967–8)
1968		
1969	Violent troubles in Northern Ireland	
1970	Conservatives win General Election Heath Prime Minister	
1971		
1972	Northern Ireland under direct rule from London	Britain joins the Common Market
1974	Miners' strike, Two general elections, Wilson Prime Minister again	
1975	Margaret Thatcher leader of the Conservative Party	Referendum on Europe

Economy and Society	Culture and Religion	Year
	John Robinson: *Honest to God* Beatlemania	1963
	Mary Quant launches the mini-skirt	1964
Discovery of natural gas in the North Sea Abolition of death penalty	Edward Bond: *Saved* at the Royal Court Decision to convert secondary schools to comprehensives Creation of the Social Science Research Council (SSRC)	1965
Hovercraft (Cockerell, 1955) goes into operation Welsh Nationalist MP elected	Archbishop of Canterbury meets the Pope	1966
Devaluation of the pound Scottish Nationalist MP elected	Arts Laboratory	1967
Student unrest: LSE, Essex, etc. (1967–8)	Abolition of theatre censorship	1968
Age of majority brought down to 18	Isle of Wight Pop Festival	1969
Discovery of oil in North Sea Equal Pay Act	Start of Woman's Liberation Movement	1970
Decimalization of currency Industrial Relations Act		1971
	Stanley Kubrick: *A Clockwork Orange*	1972
Economic crisis: inflation and unemployment		1974
North Sea oil starts to flow	Sex Discrimination Act	1975

Bibliography

1. General works of reference

The most recent bibliographical guides are: W. H. Chaloner and R. C. Richardson (eds), *British Economic and Social History: a Bibliographical Guide*, Manchester 1976; H. J. Hanham, *Bibliography of British History 1851–1914*, London 1976; J. Altholz, *Victorian England 1837–1901*, Cambridge 1970; D. Nicholls, *Nineteenth-Century Britain*, Folkestone 1978; C. L. Mowatt, *Great Britain since 1914*, London 1971; J. Westergaard, A. Weyman and P. Wiles, *Modern British Society: a Bibliography*, 2nd edn, London 1977; G. S. Bain and G. B. Woolven, *Bibliography of British Industrial Relations*, Cambridge 1978; G. R. Elton, *Modern Historians on British History 1485–1945: a critical bibliography 1945–1969*, London 1970; Social Science Research Council, *Research in Economic and Social History*, London 1971. To which one should add the *Annual Bulletin of Historical Literature*, published each year by the Historical Association, and the lists of works on economic and social history which appears annually in the *Economic History Review*. In more specialist fields, there are the annual bibliographical lists drawn up by the *Bulletin of the Society for the study of Labour History*, the *Urban History Yearbook*, *Victorian Studies*, etc.

For historical dictionaries see: J. Brendon, *A Dictionary of British History*, London 1937; S. H. Steinberg and H. I. Evans (eds), *Steinberg's Dictionary of British History*, 2nd edn, London 1970; and of course the *Dictionary of National Biography*, Oxford. As far as the labour and working-class movement is concerned, one should add J. M. Bellamy and J. Saville (eds), *Dictionary of Labour Biography*, 5 vols, London 1972–9, F. M. Powicke and E. B. Fryde (eds), *Handbook of British Chronology*, 2nd edn, London 1961.

Statistical sources: if M. Mulhall, *Dictionary of Statistics*, 1892, is difficult to obtain, sound references are conveniently accessible in B. R. Mitchell and P. Deane, *Abstract of British Historical Statistics*, Cambridge 1962; for the more recent period, on the other hand, B. R. Mitchell and H. G. Jones, *Second Abstract of British Historical Statistics*, Cambridge 1971, is less useful. For the twentieth century, A. H. Halsey (ed.), *Trends in British Society since 1900*, London 1972, is indispensible. To which one should add, London and Cambridge Economic Service, *The British Economy Key Statistics 1900–1970*, London 1972, and A. Sillitoe, *Britain in Figures: A Handbook of Social Statistics*, 2nd edn, London 1973. Also very useful are P. Deane and W. A. Cole, *British Economic Growth 1688–1959*, 2nd edn, Cambridge 1976; C. H. Feinstein, *National Income, Expenditure and Output of the United Kingdom 1855–1965*, 2nd edn, Cambridge 1977; *British Labour Statistics: Historical Abstract 1886–1968*, London 1971. D. Butler and A. Sloman, *British Political Facts 1900–1974*, 4th edn, London 1975, covers a very wide field, as, for the nineteenth century, does C. Cook and B. Keith, *British Historical Facts 1830–1900*, London 1975. E. A. Wrigley (ed.), *Nineteenth Century Society: Essays in the Use of Quantitative Methods*, Cambridge 1972, presents a more methodological viewpoint.

For the most recent developments, consult Central Statistical Office, *Annual Abstract of Statistics*, London; Central Office of Information, *Britain: An Official Handbook*, London (annual).

HISTORY AND ENVIRONMENT

In the field of historical geography, one should note P. J. Perry, *A Geography of Nineteenth Century Britain*, London 1976; H. C. Darby (ed.), *A New Historical Geography of England After 1660*, Cambridge 1976.

In order to set the movement of society back in its context, one would do well to consult works of general English history, whether they be the elegant evocations of D. Thomson, *England in the Nineteenth Century 1815–1914*, London 1950, and *England in the Twentieth Century 1914–1963*, London 1964; H. Pelling, *Modern Britain 1885–1955*, Edinburgh 1960; or whether they be the more substantial volumes in the series 'The Oxford History of England', R. C. K. Ensor, *England 1870–1914*, Oxford 1936; A. J. P. Taylor, *English History 1914–1945*, Oxford 1965. Also to be recommended is the excellent book by C. L. Mowat, *Britain Between the Wars 1918–1940*, London 1955; as well as A. Marwick, *Britain in the Century of Total War*, London 1968.

PERIODICALS

In so far as the most interesting and the most recent contributions appear in the form of articles, this bibliography would be incomplete without mentioning the principal reviews to which the reader should turn for a deeper understanding of particular aspects of British society: *Economic History Review; Population Studies; Bulletin of the Society for the Study of Labour History; Social History; Urban History Yearbook* (formerly *Newcastle*); *Past and Present; History; English Historical Review; Historical Journal; History Workshop Journal; Victorian Studies; British Journal of Sociology; International Review of Social History;* etc.

2. Society

GENERAL TRENDS

The social history of England has recently been enriched by some excellent works. Along with G. D. H. Cole and R. Postgate, *The Common People 1746–1946*, London, 1st edn 1938, 4th edn 1962, which is now somewhat dated, one should mention three remarkable syntheses, each putting forward an original interpretation: one, E. J. Hobsbawm, *Industry and Empire*, London 1968, covers the whole period; the two others stop at the end of the nineteenth century: H. Perkin, *The Origins of Modern English Society 1780–1880*, London 1969; and S. G. Checkland, *The Rise of Industrial Society in England 1815–1885*, London 1965. J. Ryder and H. Silver, *Modern English Society: History and Structure 1850–1970*, 2nd edn, London 1977, successfully combines the historical and sociological approaches in one volume; J. Roebuck, *The Making of Modern English Society from 1850*, London 1973, on the other hand, is disappointing. As for G. M. Trevelyan, *English Social History*, London 1944, this has been entirely superseded and cannot be recommended. A clear and relatively well-informed textbook is P. Gregg, *A Social and Economic History of Britain 1760–1970*, 7th edn, London 1972. The lively evocations conjured up by W. J. Reader, *Life in Victorian England*, London 1964; R. Cecil, *Life in Edwardian England*, London 1969; and L. C. B. Seaman, *Life in Britain between the Wars*, London 1970, unfortunately have no sequel after 1939.

There is an equally rich crop of books for individual periods. For the mid-Victorian era, apart from the classics such as G. M. Young (ed.), *Early Victorian England*, 2 vols, London 1934, and *Portrait of an Age*, 2nd edn, London 1953, and A. Briggs, *Victorian People*, London 1954, G. Best has presented a brilliant analysis in *Mid-Victorian Britain 1851–1875*, London 1971. Also rich in observations are W. L. Burn, *The Age of Equipoise*, London 1964; G. Kitson Clark, *The Making of Victorian England*, London 1962, and *An Expanding Society: Britain 1830–1900*, Cambridge 1967.

For the late-Victorian and Edwardian periods, perceptive views are presented in H. M. Lynd, *England in the Eighteen-Eighties*, New York 1945, and H. Pelling, *Popular Politics and Society in Late-Victorian Britain*, London 1968. Sound analyses are given in: S. Nowell-Smith (ed.), *Edwardian England*, London 1964; D. Read, *Edwardian England: Society and Politics 1901–1915*, London 1972; P. Thompson, *The Edwardians*, London 1975.

For the twentieth century, a useful survey is M. Abrams, *The Condition of the British People 1911–1945*, London 1946. A. Marwick has specialized in a study of the changes in society following the two world wars: *The Deluge: British Society and the First World War*, 2nd edn, London 1973, *War and Social Change in the Twentieth Century*, London 1974, and *The Home Front*, London 1976. For the inter-war years, the impressionistic accounts by R. Graves and A. Hodge, *The Long Week-End: A Social History of Great Britain 1918–1939*, London 1940; R. Blythe, *The Age of Illusion: England in the Twenties and Thirties 1919–1940*, London 1963, give a good feeling of the 'Roaring Twenties' and the 'Bleak Thirties'. N. Branson, *Britain in the Nineteen Twenties*, London 1976; J. Stevenson (ed.), *Social Conditions in Britain between the Wars*, London 1976; J. Stevenson and C. Cook, *The Slump*, London 1977; S. Glynn and J. Oxborrow, *Interwar Britain*, London 1976, all provide sound accounts, while N. Branson and W. Heinemann, *Britain in the Nineteen Thirties*,

London 1971, is occasionally rather tendentious. For the Second World War, A. Calder, *The People's War*, London 1969, a rich and evocative book, should be linked with the intelligent study provided by H. Pelling, *Britain and the Second World War*, London 1970, as well as with the sound analyses of P. Addison, *The Road to 1945: British Policies and the Second World War*, London 1975. On Great Britain since 1945, the book by P. Gregg, *The Welfare State: An economic and social history of Great Britain from 1945 to the present*, London 1967, contains a wealth of information presented in a somewhat uncritical manner. One should, however, consult the more recent study by C. J. Bartlett, *History of Post-War Britain 1945–1974*, London 1977. Useful analyses can be gleaned from: M. Sissons and P. French (eds), *Age of Austerity 1945–1951*, London 1963; V. Bogdanov and R. Skidelsky (eds), *The Age of Affluence 1951–1964*, London 1970; D. McKie and C. Cook (eds), *The Decade of Disillusions: British Politics in the Sixties*, London 1972. For a severe warning against the inertia of English society, see M. Shanks, *The Stagnant Society*, 2nd edn, London 1972. A. Sampson has dissected in detail the organs of power and the structure of collective life in *Anatomy of Britain*, London 1962, and then in *New Anatomy of Britain*, London 1971. Finally a brilliant semi-historical semi-prophetic description is given in M. Young, *The Rise of the Meritocracy*, London 1958.

On the evolution of social policy – from the Poor Law to the Welfare State – one should consult the small book by M. Rose, *The Relief of Poverty 1834–1914*, London 1972, as well as the textbooks by M. Bruce, *The Coming of the Welfare State*, 4th edn, London 1968, and D. Fraser, *The Evolution of the British Welfare State*, London 1973.

TOWN AND COUNTRY

The development of agriculture has been well covered in: J. D. Chambers and G. E. Mingay, *The Agricultural Revolution 1750–1880*, London 1966; C. Orwin and E. H. Whitham, *History of British Agriculture 1846–1914*, London 1964; E. H. Whitham, *Agrarian History of England and Wales*, vol. 8: *1914–1939*, London 1978. Recent critical revisions are to be found in P. J. Perry, *British Agriculture 1875–1914*, London 1973, and *British Farming in the Great Depression 1870–1914*, Newton Abbot 1974. Lord Ernle, *English Farming Past and Present*, London, 1st edn 1912, new edn 1936, should, on the other hand, now be considered completely out of date. Valid information can still be obtained in two old French works: P. Besse, *la Crise et l'évolution de l'agriculture en Angleterre de 1875 à nos jours*, Paris 1910, and P. Flavigny, *le Régime agraire de l'Angleterre au XIXᵉ siècle*, Paris 1932. Life for the country-dweller in the second half of the nineteenth century is admirably depicted in M. K. Ashby, *Joseph Ashby of Tysoe: A Study of English Village Life 1859–1919*, Cambridge 1961. Equally to be consulted is R. Samuel (ed.), *Village Life and Labour*, London 1975.

As far as the towns are concerned, although there are a great number of monographs, there is no synthesis dealing with English urban development as a whole. For the Victorian period, three excellent works are available: A. Briggs, *Victorian Cities*, London 1963; H. J. Dyos and M. Wolff (eds), *The Victorian City*, 2 vols, London 1973; D. Olsen, *The Growth of Victorian London*, London 1976. For the twentieth century, see the detailed study by C. A. Moser and W. Scott, *British Towns: a statistical study of their social and economic differences*, London 1961. T. W. Freeman, *The Conurbations of Great Britain*, 2nd edn, Manchester 1966, deals largely with historical geography. R. Williams, *The Country and the City*, London

1973, examines the image of the town. On the environment, consult A. Sutcliffe (ed.), *Multi-Storey Living*, London 1974; and E. Gauldie, *Cruel Habitations: a History of Working Class Housing 1780–1918*, London 1974. On development and planning, W. Ashworth, *The Genesis of Modern British Town Planning*, London 1954; and G. E. Cherry, *Urban Change and Planning*, Henley 1972.

POPULATION, FAMILY AND THE CONDITION OF WOMEN

A summary of the principal demographic features can be found in E. M. Hubback, *The Population of Britain*, London 1947, and R. K. Kelsall, *Population*, 2nd edn, London 1972. The more ambitious N. Tranter, *Population since the Industrial Revolution: the Case of England and Wales*, London 1973, is useful, but raises more questions than it answers. More recent studies are presented by R. Mitchinson, *British Population Changes since 1860*, London 1977; and M. Flinn (ed.), *Scottish Population History*, London 1978. On the birth-rate and the beginnings of birth-control, there are three interesting contributions: J. A. Banks, *Prosperity and Parenthood: a study of family planning among the Victorian middle classes*, London 1954; J. A. and O. Banks, *Feminism and Family Planning in Victorian England*, Liverpool 1964; and A. McLaren, *Birth-Control in Nineteenth-Century England*, London 1978. On emigration, see N. H. Carrier and J. R. Jeffery, *External Migration 1815–1950*, London 1953.

The family has been studied in monographs by M. Anderson, *Family Structure in Nineteenth Century Lancashire*, Cambridge 1971; M. Young and P. Wilmott, *Family and Kinship in East London*, London 1957, and *Family and Class in a London Suburb*, London 1960, and in a more global way by these same two authors in *The Symmetrical Family*, London 1973; and by R. Fletcher, *The Family and Marriage in Britain*, 3rd edn, London 1973. Also to be remembered is O. R. McGregor, *Divorce in England*, London 1957, as well as the contemporary inquiry by G. Gorer, *Sex and Marriage in England Today*, London 1971. The underworld of Victorian society appears in F. Henriques, *Modern Sexuality: Prostitution and Society*, vol. III, London 1968; S. Marcus, *The Other Victorians*, London 1966; R. Pearsall, *The Worm in the Bud: the World of Victorian Sexuality*, London 1969.

On the place of women in society, the growth of contemporary neo-feminism has given rise to a whole new crop of publications. To old works dealing with the struggle for rights, such as R. Strachey, *The Cause*, London 1928, new edn 1978, and E. Reiss, *Rights and Duties of English Women: a study in law and public opinion*, London 1934, one can now add various – and variously successful – attempts at syntheses: D. M. Stenton, *The English Woman in History*, London 1957; C. Rover, *Love, Morals and the Feminists*, London 1970; S. Rowbotham, *Hidden from History*, London 1973. On the Victorian period, see: M. Hewitt, *Women and Mothers in Victorian Industry*, London 1958; D. Crow, *The Victorian Woman*, London 1971; M. Vicinus (ed.), *Suffer and Be Still: Woman in the Victorian Age*, Bloomington 1972; P. Branca, *Silent Sisterhood*, London 1975; E. Trudgill, *Madonnas and Magdalens*, London 1976. On the suffragettes, whose bibliography is constantly on the increase, one should consult: R. Fulford, *Votes for Women*, London 1957; C. Rover, *Women's Suffrage and Party Politics 1866–1914*, London 1967; A. Rosen, *Rise Up Women!*, London 1974; J. Liddington and J. Norris, *One Hand Tied Behind Us: The Rise of the Women's Suffrage Movement*, London 1978; B. Harrison, *Separate Spheres:*

The Opposition to Women's Suffrage, London 1978. Cf. also A. Marwick, *Women at War 1914–1918*, London 1977. On the political role of women, see M. Currell, *Political Woman*, London 1974.

On the position of children in society, I. Pinchbeck and M. Hewitt, *Children in British Society*, vol. 2: *From the Eighteenth Century to the Children Act 1948*, is disappointing, as it confines itself to the legal aspects of the question.

On the attitude to death, note J. Morley, *Death, Heaven and the Victorians*, London 1971; J. S. Curl, *The Victorian Celebration of Death*, Newton Abbot 1972, and the study by G. Gorer, *Death, Grief and Mourning in Contemporary Britain*, London 1965.

SOCIAL STRUCTURE AND SOCIAL CLASS

There is a great amount of information available on the development of social structures: D. C. Marsh, *The Changing Social Structure of England and Wales 1871–1961*, 2nd edn, London 1965; G. D. H. Cole, *Studies in Class Structure*, London 1955; G. D. H. Cole and M. I. Cole, *The Condition of Britain*, London 1937; G. D. H. Cole, *The Post-War Condition of Britain*, London 1956; A. M. Carr-Saunders and D. C. Jones, *A Survey of the Social Structure of England and Wales*, Oxford, 1st edn 1927, 2nd edn 1937; A. M. Carr-Saunders, D. C. Jones and C. A. Moser, *A Survey of Social Conditions in England and Wales*, Oxford 1958; D. V. Glass (ed.), *Social Mobility in Britain*, London 1954; C. J. Richardson, *Contemporary Social Mobility*, London 1977.

The land-owning aristocracy has been excellently dealt with in F. M. L. Thompson, *English Landed Society in the Nineteenth Century*, London 1963; See also G. E. Mingay, *The Gentry*, London 1978. On the power élite, interesting analyses are given in W. L. Guttsman, *The British Political Elite*, 2nd edn, London 1965; and P. Stanworth and A. Giddens (eds), *Elites and Power in British Society*, Cambridge 1974. One should refer also to J. Blondel, *Voters, Parties and Leaders*, London, 1st edn 1963, revised edn 1974; R. Rose, *Politics in England Today*, London 1974.

There is no satisfactory study of the middle classes, but none the less it is worth noting W. J. Reader, *Professional Men: the Rise of the Professional Classes in the Nineteenth Century*, London 1966; and R. Lewis and A. Maude, *The Middle Classes*, London 1949. On the Army and officers, see C. Barnett, *Britain and her Army 1509–1970*, London 1970. There is, however, no equivalent for the Navy. The rise of white-collar workers has been dealt with in: F. D. Klingender, *The Condition of Clerical Labour in Great Britain*, London 1935; D. Lockwood, *The Blackcoated Worker*, London 1958; G. S. Bain, *The Growth of White-Collar Unionism*, Oxford 1970.

On the workers, sociological studies have been written by F. Zweig, *The British Worker*, London 1952, and *The Worker in an Affluent Society*, London 1961, and above all J. Goldthorpe *et al.*, *The Affluent Worker: Industrial Attitudes and Behaviour; Political Attitudes and Behaviour; The Affluent Worker in the Class Structure*, 3 vols, Cambridge 1968–9.

The redistribution of wealth and incomes has been the subject of several studies, from the pioneering L. G. Chiozza Money, *Riches and Poverty*, London 1905; Colin Clark, *National Income 1924–1931*, London 1932, and *National Income and Outlay*, London 1937; A. L. Bowley, *Wages and Income in the United Kingdom since 1860*, Cambridge 1937; right up to the recent works by R. Titmuss, *Income Distribution and Social Change*, London 1962; B. Abel-Smith and P. Townsend, *The*

Poor and the Poorest, London 1965; T. Stark, *Distribution of Personal Income in the United Kingdom 1949–1963*, Cambridge 1972; D. Wedderburn (ed.), *Poverty, Inequality and Class Structure*, Cambridge 1974; A. B. Atkinson, *The Economics of Inequality*, London 1975; A. B. Atkinson (ed.), *Personal Distribution of Incomes*, London 1976; A. B. Atkinson and A. J. Harrison, *Distribution of Personal Wealth in Britain*, Cambridge 1978. Attempts at an overall view of contemporary society are to be found in J. Westergaard and H. Ressler, *Class in a Capitalist Society*, London 1975; and A. H. Halsey, *Change in British Society*, London 1978.

THE LABOUR MOVEMENT

Here too, the bibliography is very rich. For an introduction to the history of trade-unionism, refer to H. Pelling, *A History of British Trade Unionism*, 3rd edn, London 1976; and J. Lovell and B. C. Roberts, *A Short History of the TUC*, London 1968. On a more detailed level, alongside traditional interpretations – S. and B. Webb, *The History of Trade Unionism*, London 1920 edn; G. D. H. Cole, *A Short History of the British Working-Class Movement 1789–1947*, London 1948; A. L. Morton and G. Tate, *The British Labour Movement 1770–1920*, London 1956 – one can find new points of view and new data in: A. Briggs and J. Saville (eds), *Essays in Labour History*, 3 vols, London 1960–77; E. J. Hobsbawm, *Labouring Men*, London 1964; T. Tholfsen, *Working-Class Radicalism in Mid-Victorian England*, London 1976; R. Harrison, *Before the Socialists*, London 1965; A. E. Musson, *British Trade Unions 1800–1875*, London 1972; H. A. Clegg, A. Fox, A. F. Thompson, *A History of British Trade Unionism since 1889*, vol. I: *1889–1910*, Oxford 1964; D. Kynaston, *King Labour: The British Working Class 1850–1914*, London 1976; S. Lewenhak, *Women and Trade Unions*, London 1976; N. C. Solden, *Women in British Trade Unions 1874–1976*, London 1978; A. Clinton, *Trade Union Rank and File: Trade Union Councils 1900–1940*, Manchester 1977; J. Lovell, *Trade Unions 1875–1933*, London 1977.

On the development of socialist ideas and the labour movement, see: M. Beer, *A History of British Socialism*, London 1940; H. Pelling, *The Origins of the Labour Party*, 2nd edn, Oxford 1965, and *A Short History of the Labour Party*, 6th edn, London 1978; P. Adelman, *The Rise of the Labour Party 1880–1945*, London 1972; C. Brand, *The British Labour Party: a short history*, 2nd edn, Stanford 1974; R. Miliband, *Parliamentary Socialism*, 2nd edn, London 1973. On revolutionary movements and Communism, consult: W. Kendall, *The Revolutionary Movement in Britain 1900–1921*, London 1969; H. Pelling, *The British Communist Party*, 2nd edn, London 1976; and on the contemporary scene, L. Panitch, *Social Democracy and Industrial Militancy 1945–1974*, London 1976; R. Taylor, *The Fifth Estate*, London 1978.

For an overall view of the Labour and working-class movements, see F. Bédarida, 'le Socialisme en Angleterre de la fin du XVIII⁰ siècle à 1945' in J. Droz *et al.*, *Histoire générale du socialisme*, 3 vols, Paris 1972–6.

VARIOUS ASPECTS OF SOCIAL LIFE

The following works provide an insight into different aspects of living conditions, ways of life, leisure, criminality, etc.:

J. C. Drummond and A. Wilbraham, *The Englishman's Food: A History of Five*

Centuries of English Diet, 2nd edn, London 1958; J. Burnett, *Plenty and Want: A social history of diet in England from 1815 to the present day*, 2nd edn, London 1968, and *A History of the Cost of Living*, London 1969; M. and C. H. B. Quennell, *A History of Everyday Things in England*, vol. IV: *1851–1914*, 5th edn, London 1950; vol. V: *1914–1968*, by S. E. Ellacott, London 1968; B. Harrison, *Drink and the Victorians*, London 1971; J. J. Tobias, *Crime and Industrial Society in the XIXth Century*, London 1967; J. A. R. Pimlott, *The Englishman's Holiday*, London 1947; J. Walvin, *Leisure and Society 1830–1950*, London 1978; J. K. Walton, *The Blackpool Landlady*, London 1978.

3. The economy

Three works stand out from the collection of economic histories of England: P. Mathias, *The First Industrial Nation*, London 1969, which covers the eighteenth century to 1939; W. Ashworth, *An Economic History of England 1870–1939*, London 1960; S. Pollard, *The Development of the British Economy 1914–1967*, 2nd edn, London 1969. J. H. Clapham, *An Economic History of Modern Britain*, 3 vols, Cambridge 1926–38 (vol. II: *1850–1886*; vol. III: *1886–1929*), remains an outstanding classic. More concentrated is W. H. B. Court, *A Concise Economic History of Britain from 1750 to Recent Times*, Cambridge 1954. Equally notable is the useful contribution made by D. H. Aldcroft and H. W. Richardson, *The British Economy 1870–1939*, London 1969. Contributions to the new economic history can be found in D. N. McCloskey (ed.), *Essays on a Mature Economy: Britain after 1840*, London 1971. An excellent synthesis is F. Cronzet, *L'économie de la Grande Bretagne victorienne*, Paris 1978 (English translation forthcoming).

Taking each period separately: J. D. Chambers, *The Workshop of the World 1820–1880*, London 1961, and R. Church, *The Great Victorian Boom 1851–1873*, London 1975, deal with the great expansion of the nineteenth century. From 1870 on, consult S. B. Saul, *The Myth of the Great Depression 1873–1896*, London 1969; R. S. Sayers, *A History of Economic Change in England 1880–1939*, London 1967.

On the First World War and its consequences, and on the inter-war years, see A. S. Milward, *The Economic Consequences of the Two World Wars on Britain*, London 1970; and B. W. E. Alford, *Depression and Recovery? British Economic Growth 1919–1939*, London 1970. (Both these works seriously call into question the views put forward by A. Siegfried, *la Crise britannique au XX*ᵉ *siècle*, Paris 1931.) On the problems of growth in the twentieth century, consult G. A. Philips and R. T. Maddock, *The Growth of the British Economy 1918–1968*, London 1973; and A. J. Youngson, *Britain's Economic Growth 1920–1966*, 2nd edn, London 1968.

For the period after 1945, see J. Leruez, *Economic Planning and Politics 1945–1974*, London 1975. The most recent data can be found in A. R. Prest and D. J. Coppock (eds), *The United Kingdom Economy: a Manual of Applied Economics*, 7th edn, London 1978.

Certain areas of economic life have been the subject of specialist studies. On the relationship between private enterprise and the State in the nineteenth century, it would be of benefit to consult the small books by A. J. Taylor, *Laissez-faire and State intervention in Nineteenth-Century Britain*, London 1972, and P. L. Payne, *British Entrepreneurship in the Nineteenth Century*, London 1974. On twentieth-century industry, see G. C. Allen, *The Structure of Industry in Britain*, 3rd edn, London 1970. Several sound works trace the development of transport: T. C. Barker and C. I. Savage, *An Economic History of Transport in Britain*, 3rd edn, London 1975;

H. J. Dyos and D. H. Aldcroft, *British Transport: an Economic Survey*, Leicester 1969; P. S. Bagwell, *The Transport Revolution since 1770*, London 1974.

4. Religion

A brief but relevant outline is given in A. Vidler, *The Church in an Age of Revolution*, London 1961. On the nineteenth century, L. E. Elliott-Binns, *Religion in the Victorian Era*, London 1936, remains valid, but O. Chadwick has produced an outstanding work in *The Victorian Church*, 2 vols, London 1966–1970. One should also mention A. D. Gilbert, *Religion and Society in Industrial England 1740–1914*, London 1976; and E. R. Norman, *Church and Society in England 1770–1970*, London 1976. Interesting suggestions are given in H. Davies, *Worship and Theology in England*, vol. IV: *From Newman to Martineau 1850–1900*, and vol. V: *The Ecumenical Century 1900–1965*, Princeton 1962–5. On the twentieth century, a useful but awkward work is G. S. Spinks, *Religion in Britain since 1900*, London 1952, and one should also consult K. Slack, *The British Churches Today*, London 1970. Two original works are to be recommended, one social, K. S. Inglis, *Churches and the Working Classes in Victorian England*, London 1963, the other geographical, J. D. Gay, *The Geography of Religion in England*, London 1971. More recent studies are S. Budd, *Varieties of Unbelief 1850–1960*, London 1977; and R. Currie, A. D. Gilbert, and L. S. Horsley, *Churches and Churchgoers*, Oxford 1978.

On Anglicanism, there are three books written from the Anglican point of view: S. C. Carpenter, *Church and People 1798–1889*, London 1933; J. W. C. Wand, *Anglicanism in History and Today*, London 1961; R. B. Lloyd, *The Church of England 1900–1965*, London 1966.

On the Nonconformists, see an introduction by H. Davis, *The English Free Churches*, 2nd edn, London 1963, and E. A. Payne, *The Free Church Tradition in the Life of England*, London 1944. More recently, a critical light has been shed on the subject by S. Koss, *Nonconformity and Modern British Politics*, London 1975.

Catholicism has mainly been dealt with by Catholic writers: D. Mathew, *Catholicism in England*, 2nd edn, London 1948; G. A. Beck (ed.), *The English Catholics 1850–1950*, London 1950; and in French, J. A. Lesourd, *Le Catholicisme dans la société anglaise 1765–1865*, 2 vols, Lille, 1978.

Works on religious sociology proliferate. Two works of synthesis should be noted: B. R. Wilson, *Religion in Secular Society*, London 1966, and D. Martin, *A Sociology of English Religion*, London 1967; and three good monographs: on Sheffield, E. R. Wickham, *Church and People in an Industrial City*, London 1957; on London, H. McLeod, *Class and Religion in the Late Victorian City*, London 1974; on Reading, S. Yeo, *Religious Organisations in Crisis*, London 1976.

5. Education

The institutional aspects are dealt with in J. W. Adamson, *English Education 1789–1902*, Cambridge 1930, a compact and classic book, and in S. J. Curtis, *History of Education in England*, 7th edn, London 1967, *Education in Britain since 1900*, London 1952, and, in collaboration with M. E. A. Boultwood, *An Introductory History of English Education since 1800*, 4th edn, London 1966. H. C. Barnard, *A History of English Education from 1760*, 2nd edn, London 1961, gives a clear and precise introduction to the subject. The social aspects are treated more extensively by J. Lawson and H. Silver, *A Social History of Education in England*, London 1973, and by D. Wardle, *English Popular Education 1780–1975*, Cambridge 1975. Note also: W. H. G. Armytage, *Four Centuries of English Education*, Cambridge 1964; J. Murphy, *Church, State and Schools in Britain 1800–1970*, London 1971; P. Horn, *Education in Rural England 1800–1914*, London 1978; H. C. Dent, *Education in England and Wales*, London 1977; I. G. Fenwick, *The Comprehensive School 1944–1970*, London 1976; W. K. Richmond, *Education in Britain since 1944*, London 1978.

On public schools, see T. W. Bamford, *The Rise of the Public Schools*, London 1967; and D. Newsome, *Godliness and Good Learning*, London 1961.

On teachers, note A. Tropp, *The School Teachers*, London 1957.

An excellent book on adult education and popular culture is J. F. C. Harrison, *Learning and Living 1790–1960: a study in the history of the English adult education movement*, London 1961.

6. Culture

Besides R. Williams' stimulating studies, *Culture and Society 1780–1950*, London 1958, and *The Long Revolution*, London 1961, one should consult the various studies on prevailing attitudes and values. In particular, for the Victorian period, see: *Ideas and Beliefs of the Victorians*, BBC Talks, London 1949; W. E. Houghton, *The Victorian Frame of Mind*, New Haven, Conn. 1957; and R. D. Altick, *Victorian People and Ideas*, New York 1973. On the dominant culture and popular literature, refer to R. D. Altick, *The English Common Reader: a social history of the mass reading-public 1800–1900*, Chicago 1957; and M. Vicinus, *The Industrial Muse*, London 1975.

For the twentieth century, there is an interesting contribution from S. Hynes, *The Edwardian Turn of Mind*, Princeton 1968; and one should also consult the small descriptive encyclopaedia by C. B. Cox and A. E. Dyson (eds), *The Twentieth Century Mind: History, Ideas and Literature in Britain 1900–1965*, 3 vols, London 1972. On the working-class world, R. Hoggart, *The Uses of Literacy*, London 1957, is a first-class book. Also to be recommended is the study by G. Gorer, *Exploring English Character*, London 1955. On youth and the counter-culture, see F. Musgrove, *Youth and the Social Order*, London 1964, and *Ecstasy and Holiness: Counter Culture and the Open Society*, London 1975; and S. Hall and T. Jefferson, *Resistance through Rituals: Youth Sub-cultures in Post-War Britain*, London 1977. On the political front, see B. Jessop, *Traditionalism, Conservatism and British Political Culture*, London 1974.

On the development of literature, good references are given in B. Ford (ed.), *Pelican Guide to English Literature*, vol. 6: *From Dickens to Hardy*; vol. 7: *The Modern Age*, London 1958–1961.

7. National and racial problems

Descriptions of Scottish society can be found in: R. H. Campbell, *Scotland since 1707: the Rise of an Industrial Society*, Oxford 1965; W. Ferguson, *Scotland: 1689 to the Present*, Edinburgh 1968; W. H. Marwick, *Scotland in Modern Times: An Outline of Economic and Social Development since 1707*, London 1964; C. Harvie, *Scotland and Nationalism*, London 1977; J. Brand, *The National Movement in Scotland*, London 1978.

On Wales, consult: parts of Brinley Thomas (ed.), *The Welsh Economy*, Cardiff 1962; A. Butt Philip, *The Welsh Question: Nationalism in Welsh Politics 1945–1970*, Cardiff 1976; D. Williams, *A History of Modern Wales*, London 1977.

Attempts at an overall view are presented in M. Hexter, *Internal Colonialism: The Celtic Fringe in British National Development 1536–1966*, London 1975; A. H. Birch, *Political Integration and Disintegration in the British Isles*, London 1978; and V. Bogdanov, *Devolution*, London 1979.

Whilst earlier immigration has been studied by J. A. Jackson, *The Irish in Britain*, London 1963, and L. P. Gartner, *The Jewish Immigrant in England 1870—1914*, London 1960 (note here too the relevant book by V. D. Lipman, *Social History of the Jews in England 1850–1950*, London 1954), and C. Holmes, *Anti-Semitism in Britain 1876–1939*, London 1979, coloured immigration from the 1950s on has given rise to a multitude of studies: E. J. B. Rose (ed.) *Colour and Citizenship: A Report on British Race Relations*, London 1969 (a detailed study); C. S. Hill, *Immigration and Integration: A study of the settlement of coloured minorities in Britain*, Oxford 1970 (precise and practical textbook); E. Krausz, *Ethnic Minorities in Britain*, London 1971 (a useful panorama); C. Holmes (ed.), *Immigrants and Minorities in British Society*, London 1978.

8. Foreign views: the English seen by the French

One should be very careful not to overlook the precious mine of information available in the accounts of the French who have stayed some time in England, whether simply as travellers, or else intending to work on some more detailed research, or even, because, wanted by the police in their own country, they sought refuge there (such as Martin Nadaud, Alfred Esquiros, Jules Vallès). A great many of these publications, made up of observations and impressions drawn from daily life, of reports and studies, cannot fail to be highly instructive about English society (unfortunately, since the Second World War, the seam has run out). Amongst the generations of visitors who thus succeeded one another, one should mention: at the beginning of the Victorian era, Flora Tristan, *Promenades dans Londres*, 1840, republished with an introduction by F. Bédarida, Paris 1978; Léon Faucher, *Etudes sur l'Angleterre*, 1845; and the illustrations of Gavarni. From the middle of the century, Léonce de Lavergne, *Essai sur l'Économie rurale de l'Angleterre*, 1854; Hector Malot, *la Vie Moderne en Angleterre*, 1862; Martin Nadaud, *Histoire des classes ouvrières en Angleterre*, 1872; A. Esquiros, *l'Angleterre et la vie anglaise*, 1869; Taine, *Notes sur l'Angleterre*, 1872; and Gustave Doré's realistic illustrations of London. In the 1880s, there are the writings of Jules Vallès, *la Rue à Londres*, 1884; and Max O'Rell (Paul Blouet), *John Bull et son île*, 1883. At the turn of the century, one finds: Paul de Rousiers, *la Question ouvrière en Angleterre*, 1895, and *le Trade-unionisme en Angleterre*, 1897; E. Boutmy, *Psychologie politique du peuple anglais au XIXe siècle*, 1901; Jacques Bardoux, *Psychologie de l'Angleterre contemporaine*, 3 vols, 1906–13, and *l'Ouvrier anglais aujourd'hui*, 1921. The inter-war years are represented by André Siegfried, André Philip, Pierre Bourdan: the last of which, *Perplexités et Grandeur de l'Angleterre*, published 1945 (in English, Pierre Maillaud, *The English Way*) represents the last noteworthy study in this long series.

Note, too, two collections made by particularly acute observers of social development in England: *Marx and Engels on Britain*, Moscow 1962, and *Lenin on Britain*, Moscow 1959.

Index